THE
TRUE
HEAVEN

THE TRUE HEAVEN

not what you thought

better than you expected

Joe Beam & Lee Wilson

LEAFWOOD
PUBLISHERS
Abilene, Texas

THE TRUE HEAVEN

NOT WHAT YOU THOUGHT, BETTER THAN YOU EXPECTED

L E A F W O O D
P U B L I S H E R S

Copyright 2010 by Joe Beam & Lee Wilson

ISBN 978-0-89112-643-0
LCCN 2010004756

Printed in the United States of America

Scripture quotations, unless otherwise noted, are from The Holy Bible,
New International Version. Copyright 1984, International Bible Society.
Used by permission of Zondervan Publishers.

LIBRARY OF CONGRESS CATALOGING-IN-PUBLICATION DATA
Beam, Joe.
  The true heaven : not what you thought, better than you expected / Joe Beam & Lee Wilson.
      p. cm.
  Rev. ed. of: The real heaven.
  1. Heaven--Christianity. 2. Heaven--Biblical teaching. I. Wilson, Lee, 1980- II. Beam, Joe. Real
heaven. III. Title.
  BT846.3.B435 2010
  236'.24--dc22

                                                                                    2010004756

Cover design by Rick Gibson
Interior text design by Sandy Armstrong

Leafwood Publishers
1626 Campus Court
Abilene, Texas 79601
1-877-816-4455 toll free

For current information about all Leafwood titles, visit our Web site:
www.leafwoodpublishers.com

10 11 12 13 14 15 / 7 6 5 4 3 2 1

Contents

Dedication

For those who have died in Christ and because of him will live again.

Acknowledgements

Joe Would Like to Thank...

Thanks to my wife Alice and my daughters, Angel, Joanna, and Kimberly for their loving commitment and continuing support.

I'm also very grateful to the staff at LovePath International for working to change the world through strengthening marriages and families.

Lee Would Like to Thank...

Special thanks to my wife Joanna and our sons, Jacob and Tyler, for their patience during the writing of this book when "family time" often happened while I was in another room pecking on my computer. I love you all more than life itself.

Thanks to my dad and mom for their love and for raising me in a home where the Bible was the text book for life. If not for them, I likely would not ever see heaven. I love you more than words can say.

Thanks to my brother, Josh, for his service to the world as a soldier in the United States Navy. If not for his selflessness, and the service of others like him such as my dad and grandpa, I might not have the freedom to express my opinions in a book such as this. Thank you!

Thanks to my grandmothers, Marie Stamps and Empress Wilson, for being powerful examples of Jesus Christ, and to my grandfathers, Laymond Stamps and Paul Wilson, for showing me that the best sermon is a life of integrity, courage, and smiles while walking humbly with God.

Thanks to my in-laws, Joe, Alice, Angel, and Kimberly. Being family with you is beyond simply "law." Thank you for making me a real part of your family.

Additionally, thank you, Joe, for inviting me to be part of this book. It is an honor to write with my favorite writer.

INTRODUCTION

An Explanation of How Dread Turned to Hope

JOE BEAM

For years I thought I was the only one. I kept it quiet, like some nasty secret that will haunt and humiliate you if others find out. I even wondered if it might be heresy, that maybe God himself was thoroughly disgusted with me. One thing was sure: if God had written me off because of this, then I wouldn't have to be afraid any longer because what I feared wasn't going to happen.

You see, I was terrified by the entire concept of heaven.

I'd read enough, heard enough sermons, and even preached some of my own about the terrors of hell, so I was absolutely convinced I wanted nothing to do with that place. But to me, the opposite choice was almost as scary. Living in a place for eternity, singing or worshipping or whatever they do up there with no endings, transitions, or changes? I couldn't see how anyone would want to be in a place like that, especially one that was never, ever going to end. I felt trapped; it was either that or hell, and I wanted neither of them.

There were days when the idea of complete annihilation appealed more to me.

Once I tried talking to another minister about it. I hoped he would give me some insight that would clear my mind, heal my fear, and give me a peace about the next life that I had given to so many others when death came knocking.

Oh, I knew the right words to say to a dying person and to his family, and I could speak them convincingly. I actually believed them. They gave comfort to the people to whom I ministered, but they made my *own* fears worse.

So, over coffee, with no small amount of emotion, I poured my trepidation out on the table and waited for him to set me straight and end my apprehension. His reply? "Well, personally, I really look forward to heaven." And that was that. He never mentioned it again.

The only other time I gave it a try was with a man who is a true shepherd in the kingdom of God. He has helped so many people in so many ways that I decided to risk it once again. I summoned enough courage to tell him about my fear. He replied, "I feel the same way. Dying and going to heaven forever scares me beyond my ability to explain. I've tried to figure it out and think that maybe it's the idea of having no control over my life or choices or anything else. I don't want to live like a robot."

I listened carefully, wondering if that's what drove my fears, but found nothing in his words that gave me any understanding of myself, and nothing that diminished my emotional turmoil. Maybe there was some small comfort in finding a fellow sufferer, but there wasn't even a hint of a cure.

I never shared my own fears again, at least not that I can remember; but I began to listen carefully as others talked about heaven. To my surprise, I wasn't the only one who wasn't excited about going there. More and more, I heard Christians who loved God and lived godly lives mention their fear of eternity in heaven. One brother said, "You people who like to sing will enjoy it there. I don't get into worship like you do and can't imagine I'll be happy doing that for eternity." Others made statements that were nearly as bold as the emotions I felt.

Don't think that I spent inordinate amounts of time thinking about death and the life beyond. It hardly ever came to mind. It's just that when it did, I felt this churning in the pit of my stomach and almost a panic that every day I was closer to facing this than I had ever been before. Maybe a couple of times a year it would come sneaking into my thoughts. I'd be depressed for several hours and then not think of it again for months on end. It wasn't as if I was obsessed; most of the time it just didn't exist for me.

There *were* things about heaven that really attracted me. I could even talk about heaven in regard to my loved ones who'd gone on and feel happy for them. I would sometimes think of how heaven is going to be a very different existence for my mentally handicapped daughter, Angel. She won't be "different" there. I looked forward to having conversations with her that I can never have here because of her lack of understanding.

It's just the idea of living there *forever* that made my blood run cold.

Jerry Rushford was kind enough to invite me to speak at the Annual Bible Lectures at Pepperdine University in Malibu, California. When he asked me for a topic, I decided to speak on the life to come. For the three lectures, I spoke once on where the dead are, once on what hell is like, and once on what heaven is like.

I presented those lectures in May 2004. My only regret is that I hadn't prepared them a long time before. As I researched, studied, and meditated, I learned that my concept of heaven was far from the mark. It *will* last forever; that part is true. But it isn't just standing around singing forever and ever and ever. Nor is it a life that is so unlike this life that we have no way to relate or anticipate its joys.

Heaven is a new life. A better life, to be sure, but a life that in many ways is like the life we live here. It has relationships, variety, excitement, and emotional fulfillment. We won't be regimented robots but will have the ability to think, choose, and act.

That's what we want to show you in this book. My son-in-law, Lee Wilson, co-authored this book with me. He brings a unique perspective on God's Word and life, and his involvement makes this a better book than it would have been otherwise.

Are we Bible scholars? By no means. Just a couple of guys trying to understand Scripture and put it into effect in our lives.

Do we have all the answers? Obviously not. We aren't shy about sharing our views, but we admit that they are just that—our views. Our goal isn't to get you to agree with everything; it is to get you to think. Feel free to disagree, to ask your own questions. Our hope is that groups of Christians—or anyone else interested in what happens after human death—will use this book as a starter for Bible study, discussion, and lively debate.

As for me and thousands—if not millions—like me, I'm happy to be happy about heaven rather than dreading it.

Are you ready for an adventure? Ready to have your thoughts on heaven challenged, maybe even changed? Ready to get excited about the place that awaits those who love God? Well, for the first time in my life, I *am* excited! By the time you finish this study, I think you might be, too.

Oh, one last thing. Rather than using the clumsy "Joe thinks this" and "Lee thinks that," we simply speak in one voice. The "I" and "me" in this book represent two people. Does that mean we always agree? No! It is simply a writing style that we have chosen. Our debates will continue for a lifetime. (He's rather hardheaded, you understand . . . and, so am I.) So as you read stories of people in this book, remember that we usually do not distinguish Joe's story from Lee's. Sometimes a story doesn't come from either of us specifically but is a melding of stories from similar experiences. As in all my books, I attempt to protect the identity of most people mentioned by disguising details. If a person's first and last name is used, that story is specifically about that person. If you don't see your name in a story, then rest easy. It isn't about you.

CHAPTER 1
The Myth of Heaven

Can't say I've heard very many sermons about heaven, but I've heard plenty about hell. The problem is that the talks I did hear about heaven were just about as scary as the ones about hell.

One of the few discussions I remember my youth group having about heaven was so unnerving that we never brought it up again. We didn't want to hear or even think about it if that's what heaven was like. Though I hate to say it, in some ways it sounded more like death than hell itself.

The youth minister and his volunteers concluded that we'd be spirits singing hymns forever in heaven. Nothing else. For those of us who really loved God, we were told, that should be wonderful news. None of us really had the courage to say what we thought about such wonderful news. I could tell by the looks on the faces in the circle surrounding me that we were all thinking the same thing, and all trying not to think it.

"That's it? That sounds awful!"

We loved God. We wanted to love God more and grow in our faith, but is *that* really our reward for being the "good" kids, taking purity pledges, wearing WWJD bracelets, and "just saying no"?

Then came the knockout punch to smack us into reality. We'd better learn to love that idea of heaven because hell was the only alternative. That, somehow, seemed to make the eternal-old-folks-ghost-choir idea all the more wonderful to the adults teaching us.

I confess that in my teenage years I sometimes felt that I'd better live life and have my adventures while I could because heaven was going to be as much fun as Bingo night at the nursing home. Surely something was wrong with me because I actually really liked living on earth most of the time. I enjoyed summer nights at the river with friends, cookouts, food, sports, movies, a good book, my dog, and birthday parties. What kind of sick, spiritually depraved person was I to actually wish I could have those things in heaven? Maybe if I loved God more those things would become boring to me. Maybe if I sat in my room and prayed all day God would make it so that I actually wanted to be a bodiless spook singing all verses of "Lily of the Valley" for eternity.

On one occasion, a preacher stepped up to the pulpit after our congregation had sung several hymns and said, "Well, if you didn't like that then you're not going to like heaven 'cause that's what we're going to be doing forever."

I guess he thought he was motivating us.

I remember thinking: yes, I liked some of the songs, but I honestly didn't want to sit in a worship service for a billion years! I remember thinking that if only Eve hadn't messed it up for all of us then I'd be in a beautiful Garden of Eden nature scene skipping rocks across the lake, working on my tan, and flirting with some pretty girl, but now I'm going to die one day and be forced to sit in church forever!

Maybe you can relate to the frustration I experienced. It's possible that you were never taught that view of heaven, but the odds are that you were. If so, then perhaps like me you've been afraid to think about heaven because you knew you were supposed to like it, but most things you heard about it really just depressed you.

But that all changed for me.

I finally came to understand that I had believed a myth about heaven rather than a truth about heaven. I held a view of heaven that not only colossally underestimated God, but also possibly turned people away from him.

My new understanding of heaven began by simply opening the Bible and studying what it says about God's plans for his children after death. I recall at that time how much more clear the Bible was in describing heaven than I had always assumed it was. In the past I had purposefully given little attention to passages that discussed heaven because I thought it was beyond our ability to understand or that it was simply figurative. I decided that heaven would be good and God would take care of it. While both of those things are true, as with other theological topics, we are told to study and seek God through his Word. "Do your best to present yourself to God as one approved, a workman who does not need to be ashamed and who correctly handles the word of truth"

(2 Timothy 2:15). "God looks down from heaven on the sons of men to see if there are any who understand, any who seek God" (Psalm 53:2).

God wants us to seek him and his truth. His kingdom is extremely important to him and to us and, therefore, educating ourselves on it is important. We'll be discussing that in more detail later in this book, but just know that I believe that we should seek God and not give up when certain matters confuse us.

Though I don't have all the answers—and maybe don't have the answers I think I have!—I urge folks to rethink the common concept of heaven. I am a Bible student. I ask questions. I seek answers. In this book, I share some of the questions that intrigue me and the answers I've come to so far. It's up to you to decide if I am correct or not. I pray that you will be stimulated to ask your own questions and to see what God actually wishes us to know about heaven.

The Message of Heaven Is for All Ages

With the graying of America, it seems natural that people would be thinking more about what comes after death. But heaven isn't just an "old geezers" topic, but also one of great interest to every age and nation. In a world of terrorists, gangs, AIDS, cancer, flu epidemics, nuclear weapons, and natural disasters, many people want answers to two essential questions: 1. Is death the end? 2. If there is another life, what will it be like?

Furthermore, we currently see strong interest in the supernatural and immortality among the young, considering the runaway success of stories like *Twilight*, Buffy, Harry Potter, and others. We would better serve everyone by providing information about eternal life and real supernatural creatures like angels instead of just fictional stories about immortal vampires.

God created humans for eternal life and I believe the reason the topic has become so popular is that we naturally crave such life. We desire eternal life because God originally created us to live forever. Jesus was resurrected to live forever and offers the same life to us. That should be our message to the world. Rather than living vicariously through vampires and other fictional immortals portrayed in movies and books, God offers us real eternal life. That is the message we need to share.

We presented our first seminar on heaven to a medium-sized church with a large youth group. The minister who invited us to speak asked if we wanted the youth group in the class. I told him we did and he seemed excited about that. But a few days later the youth minister sent word that he had decided not to bring the youth group in because he thought the topic would be too deep. In addition, he didn't want to break the routine of their teen-only worship service on the other side of the building.

I understood the teens wanting to have devotional time together, but I felt so strongly about the topic that I urged the youth minister to bring the teens to hear us teach about heaven, at least for the first session.

He grudgingly brought the group in for the first session. Afterwards the teens practically mobbed me with questions. They were completely fascinated. However, the youth minister wasn't as excited, "It went . . . okay," he said. "But we'll be in our usual contemporary worship on the other side of the building next week."

The next week we started the session with no teens. It was obvious because they had taken up nearly an entire side of the auditorium the week before. A few minutes into the session we saw the teens walk in. First in a group of five, then ten, then twenty, and finally all of them came through the doors and grabbed a seat.

Later I asked one of the teens what happened. She said that the youth minister had begun their usual separate service, but one of the girls had asked why they weren't in our heaven seminar. The youth minister explained that he wanted them back in their regular routine.

The girl asked, "What if we want to hear the heaven class?"

The youth minister seemed a little irritated, but said that if they wanted to hear it again, they could. The entire group left!

It turns out that these teenagers wanted to know what they were committing their lives to and where the gospel would ultimately take them. They were asking themselves the very real question, "What comes after this?" They had been taught that good little boys and girls give their lives to Jesus so that they will go to heaven one day. Well, if that was the case, what was this heaven going to be like?

The message of the Bible is more than just that Jesus can save us from hell; it's that he can give us heaven! We seem so easily convinced that God has the power to make a terrible place to punish us beyond our worst nightmares; but many seem to struggle to believe God could make a place for us that would fulfill, thrill, and excite us beyond our greatest dreams.

If we want heaven to mean anything, don't we need to develop a better understanding of heaven? Perhaps it would be good if we Christians reexamined our basic ideas about heaven.

"We Can't Know What Heaven Will Be Like."

Try replacing that thought with the opposite statement: We *can* know what heaven will be like.

Admittedly, it isn't possible to understand completely something that we have not yet experienced. For example, no matter how well astronauts describe what it was like to walk on earth's moon, we can never really comprehend that experience without having it. It doesn't even have to be that exotic. We hear people try to describe for us some experience they had only to discover that to the uninitiated it is indescribable. "You just had to be there." But that doesn't mean that we can't get at least a picture of what the person is trying to communicate.

Astronauts had the advantage of video. While I haven't been to the moon, at least I saw the pictures and that makes it more understandable for me. Unfortunately, until the recent rise of ever-present video devices (anyone have a cell phone?), the world has had to rely on verbal and written descriptions. The teller/writer chooses words and scenes to which we can relate to draw the image of what we have not yet experienced. Though word pictures can be quite vivid, they are painted on the landscape of the imagination. As each of us listens to or reads the same description, we "see" different representations of that description. While that is far from perfect in helping us understand, it is adequate to get the basics.

For example, if we were telling a person who had never seen an airplane soar through the skies that it is "sort of like a bird that carries people," our vastly inadequate explanation in fact does communicate some of the characteristics of an airplane. The hearer doesn't comprehend completely the idea of a silver tube full of people sailing across the sky, but at least he understands that it does indeed fly and that it somehow transports people.

Think of that concept as we read this description in Revelation 21:18-21:

> The wall was made of jasper, and the city of pure gold, as pure as glass. The foundations of the city walls were decorated with every kind of precious stone. The first foundation was jasper, the second sapphire, the third chalcedony, the fourth emerald, the fifth sardonyx, the sixth carnelian, the seventh chrysolite, the eighth beryl, the ninth topaz, the tenth chrysoprase, the eleventh jacinth, and the twelfth amethyst. The twelve gates were twelve pearls, each gate made of a single pearl. The great street of the city was of pure gold, like transparent glass.

Just before this passage, John gave the dimensions of the Holy City as 12,000 stadia long, wide, and high. That's about 1,400 miles in every direction, including up. A perfect cube. By the way, that 1,400 mile high wall is also 200 feet thick. Hmm. Let's see now, that would make heaven's main floor 1,960,000 square miles, but then we could add a floor every ten feet for another 1,400 miles which gives us another 739,200 floors, and we come up with a total floor space of....

That kind of logic misses the point, don't you think?

Do the words of Revelation comprise a detailed and accurate representation of heaven, or are they pictures that we can relate to in order to give us an idea? It is reasonable to understand descriptions of streets of gold and all the other wonderful imagery of heaven as representing heaven rather than specifically describing heaven. The words give us an idea, similar to the way a bird represents an airplane. Don't misunderstand: I'm not emphatically stating that there are no gold streets in heaven, but I am saying that I'm not sure that is the intent of the description. God describes for us a place beyond our experience or imagination by comparing it to things that we can understand on some level. Gold streets? That provides the thought that heaven is a place far better than any I've visited so far. A place without poverty. A richer experience than I've ever lived. It doesn't matter to me if "streets of gold" is a symbol or a specific reality. My guess is that the phrase describes heaven with words I can understand to give me a not-so-clear yet exciting view of what I do not understand.

By reading through the "pictures" of the life to come, including those descriptions of what God intends to do with this earth and his promised New Heaven and New Earth, we learn of his intentions. Consider the following passage:

Then I saw a new heaven and a new earth, for the first heaven and the first earth had passed away, and there was no longer any sea. I saw the Holy City, the new Jerusalem, coming down out of heaven from God, prepared as a bride beautifully dressed for her husband. And I heard a loud voice from the throne saying, "Now the dwelling of God is with men, and he will live with them. They will be his people, and God himself will be with them and be their God." (Revelation 21:1-3)

Through this and many other passages, we can understand enough about heaven to know what it is like, at least in the broad sense. Not perfectly, of course, because we haven't been there. But enough to understand what lies in store for those who are heaven bound—and enough to help us eliminate the myths and clichés about heaven that we have assumed are true.

"We'll Just Be Worshipping God There Forever."

Typically, this statement pictures throngs of people surrounding God's throne, singing day and night forever and ever in something similar to a church song service. Try replacing that picture with a different picture of what it means to worship God forever. While gathering around the throne singing forever sounds very spiritual, worship is much broader than just singing.

Worship encompasses many things, including living for God and doing things to serve others. "Therefore, I urge you, brothers, in view of

God's mercy, to offer your bodies as living sacrifices, holy and pleasing to God—this is your spiritual act of worship" (Romans 12:1). "Through Jesus, therefore, let us continually offer to God a sacrifice of praise—the fruit of lips that confess his name. And do not forget to do good and to share with others, for with such sacrifices God is pleased" (Hebrews 13:15-16).

Will we indeed live our lives for God and do things for others when we are in heaven? Yes. Just as our worship here is more than singing and praying, our worship there will be as well. In heaven, life will go on as God originally designed it to go on here. No sickness, pain, or dying, but also a lot more than singing our hearts out. Think in terms of cities, homes, transportation, and relationships as they could have been here had our ancestors not transgressed in the garden. As you will see from this study, there will be far more to our activities in heaven than singing nonstop for eternity.

Heretical?

Back in the 1970s, I listened at length to a minister expounding on the brilliance of biblical scholar Robert Shank. His two books, *Life in the Son* and *Elect in the Son*, addressed topics close to that minister's heart. Shank waded into the arguments between Calvinists and Arminians—predestination versus free will—and made the Arminians very happy. However, the same minister who had babbled on about Shank's wisdom had a different story the next time we met. It would be my first lesson in how those who sing hosannas to a person early in the week may shout for his execution come Friday. He had read Shank's new book, *God's Tomorrow*, which was about life after death. As I recall, that book turned many Shank fans into witch hunters.

The only thing I remember about the minister's attack is that he was tremendously offended by Shank's belief that in the next life he would continue his beloved hobby of growing tomatoes. I'm sure there was more to his objection, but that one stood out because he returned to the subject repeatedly. How in the world could someone as right as Shank on other theological matters be so warped when it came to matters of the next life?

I never heard much about Shank again. He moved into other circles and continued his study and writing. Nevertheless, to the brotherhood of believers to which I belonged, he no longer had pertinence. Tomatoes in heaven were just too heretical. We forgot the poor, misguided soul and moved on.

Though I remember little of my own reaction to Shank's purported beliefs at the time, I likely wrote him off as did the others in my fellowship. I wish I hadn't. Not only have I come to the view that Shank may grow his tomatoes in the New Heaven and Earth, I believe I'll get to have a tomato sandwich with him someday. I'll travel in some sort of conveyance and will enjoy the food that we share. I'll taste it, relish it, and look forward to the next meal, as well as to all the other activities of life on an earth recreated to be what God designed it to be in the first place.

Ready to begin our study?

As we do, please note this. In my previous books, such as *Seeing the Unseen*, I approach subjects in greater detail and with more explanation. The study of heaven is, at least to some degree, speculative in that the scriptural language used to describe it is often caged in such beautiful imagery. Don't worry; in this book I provide many Scriptures to read and think about. However, unlike a work for scholars, I do little in depth exegesis of those passages. Again, I don't write to give all the answers; I write to raise the questions. I share my views, but I hope that they do not come across as dogmatic. Particularly on this subject, we are all learners.

Heaven Is an Actual Place

CHAPTER 2

"Heaven is a state of mind!" he emphasized to his audience. "You're situation will never be perfect, so you must learn to *choose* happiness and contentment!"

Perhaps you've heard self-help gurus use similar words to encourage positive thinking. It sounds familiar, doesn't it? In Philippians 4:11, Paul says, "I have learned to be content whatever the circumstances."

However, that is *not* the same as heaven.

The Bible tells us heaven is as real as your own backyard. That means that when we are there, no one will have to convince us that we are truly experiencing heaven. We will not have to "open our minds" or "listen with our hearts" to experience it; we will know it in absolute reality. Heaven will not be some vaporous, transparent illusion. Rather, it will be a real place that can be seen, smelled, touched, heard, and tasted.

Actually, it is your own backyard. "'As the new heavens and the new earth that I make will endure before me,' declares the LORD, 'so will your name and descendants endure'" (Isaiah 66:22).

But different.

The Destruction of What Is Now

We read that God will destroy the present earth and universe because of sin's contamination. The Apostle Peter assured us this will occur and warned direly against forgetting it. He paints a terrifying picture of the power and wrath of God.

> I want you to recall the words spoken in the past by the holy prophets and the command given by our Lord and Savior through your apostles.
>
> First of all, you must understand that in the last days scoffers will come, scoffing and following their own evil desires. They will say, "Where is this 'coming' he promised? Ever since our fathers died, everything goes on as it has since the beginning of creation." But they deliberately forget that long ago by God's word the heavens existed and the earth was formed out of water and by water. By these waters also the world of that time was deluged and destroyed. By the same word the present heavens and earth are reserved for fire, being kept for the day of judgment and destruction of ungodly men.

But do not forget this one thing, dear friends: With the Lord a day is like a thousand years, and a thousand years are like a day. The Lord is not slow in keeping his promise, as some understand slowness. He is patient with you, not wanting anyone to perish, but everyone to come to repentance.

But the day of the Lord will come like a thief. The heavens will disappear with a roar; the elements will be destroyed by fire, and the earth and everything in it will be laid bare.

Since everything will be destroyed in this way, what kind of people ought you to be? You ought to live holy and godly lives as you look forward to the day of God and speed its coming. That day will bring about the destruction of the heavens by fire, and the elements will melt in the heat. (2 Peter 3:2-12)

If that were all there was to that message, I would find it most distressing. However, Peter finishes the teaching with this: "But in keeping with his promise we are looking forward to a new heaven and a new earth, the home of righteousness" (3:13)

As God destroys what we have now, he brings into existence a new reality, including a New Earth. That's right, a New Earth. Not broken like the one on which we now live. But one reborn by the power of the God who first spoke it all into existence. The Master Creator. According to the Bible, we will live in corporal bodies on a tangible sphere called earth. The New Earth. Just as those resurrected bodies will be far superior to the ones we now inhabit, the New Earth will be far superior to the one that we live on now.

Heaven is more than some ethereal essence floating somewhere above the clouds. It's not simply another dimension wildly, fantastically different from ours. It's a real place that God chose to describe not only in terms of *his* dwelling place, but also of ours. It is not just heaven to which we look; we look also for a New Earth. God's dwelling place combines with that of humankind, as Revelation 21:1-4 tells us. And God chose to make it a world to which we can relate by making it the new version of this old world that has staggered under the weight of imperfection.

In fact, the New Heavens and Earth will so overshadow the old that Isaiah 65:17 tells us the old will not even "come to mind:" "Behold, I will create new heavens and a new earth. The former things will not be remembered, nor will they come to mind. But be glad and rejoice forever in what I will create."

What is real to us now will no longer exist, but something that is *just as real* will replace what we know. We will not exist in a place that is much different from what this world originally was made to be, but rather we will exist in a reborn world that will last forever.

Heaven Is Not Just a Future Concept

When the Bible uses the word *heaven* or *heavens*, sometimes it is talking about the sky; other times, the universe; and still other times, the heaven where God reigns on his throne. Typically, Jewish people of the first century viewed the first heaven as where the birds fly. You and

I call that the atmosphere. They saw the second heaven as the place where stars exist. We call that space. The third heaven was for them the dwelling place of God. As you probably expected, the word "heaven" in the title of this book is not referring to the sky or the universe, but the heaven where God dwells and reigns on his throne.

Though a New Heaven will come, heaven exists right now. The Bible tells us that beings traveled to and from heaven and this earth. In addition to Jesus coming to earth from heaven, the Bible says angels, God's Holy Spirit, and humans traveled between the two places.

The Holy Spirit

Then John gave this testimony: "I saw the Spirit come down from heaven as a dove and remain on him. I would not have known him, except that the one who sent me to baptize with water told me, 'The man on whom you see the Spirit come down and remain is he who will baptize with the Holy Spirit.' I have seen and I testify that this is the Son of God." (John 1:32-33)

Jesus

Jesus said to them, "I tell you the truth, it is not Moses who has given you the bread from heaven, but it is my Father who gives you the true bread from heaven. For the bread of God is he who comes down from heaven and gives life to the world." (John 6:32-33)

In my former book, Theophilus, I wrote about all that Jesus began to do and to teach until the day he was taken up to heaven, after giving instructions through the Holy Spirit to the apostles he had chosen. (Acts 1:1-2)

Angels

There was a violent earthquake, for an angel of the Lord came down from heaven and, going to the tomb, rolled back the stone and sat on it. His appearance was like lightning, and his clothes were white as snow. (Matthew 28:2-4)

In Daniel 10 we read about an angel traveling for three weeks to appear to Daniel because of his prayer. The angel was detained by a battle with fallen angels, who were led by the fallen angel referred to as "the prince of the Persian kingdom" (Daniel 10:13). The angel Michael, who was referred to as "one of the chief princes," came to help so that this angel could get to Daniel with a message. This seems to suggest that both good and bad angels have had at least an occasional presence on earth. The Bible tells us that good angels traveled from heaven to earth and the fallen angels were cast to earth by God at some point in time, according to Revelation 12:9: "The great dragon was hurled down— that ancient serpent called the devil, or Satan, who leads the whole world astray. He was hurled to the earth, and his angels with him."

Humans

I know a man in Christ who fourteen years ago was caught up to the third heaven. Whether it was in the body or out of the body I do not know—God knows. And I know that this man—whether in the body or apart from the body I do not know, but God knows—was caught up to paradise. He heard inexpressible things, things that man is not permitted to tell. (2 Corinthians 12:2-4)

Heaven will not only be real to us in the future, it exists now and has been a place of activity and consciousness in the past. One of the major differences is that the heaven that is to come will combine the dwelling place of God (the New Heaven) with the dwelling place of men (the New Earth.) This forever restores complete fellowship between God and humanity.

The Master Builder at Work

I like songs and hymns written by Ira Stamphill, an Assemblies of God pastor born on Valentine's Day in 1914. I most like his 1949 classic about "a mansion just over the hilltop in that bright land where we'll never grow old." He based it on the King James Version's translation of John 14:1-3 that employed the word "mansion." Some new translations, such as the New International Version, change the word to "rooms." "Do not let your hearts be troubled. Trust in God; trust also in me. In my Father's house are many rooms; if it were not so, I would have told you. I am going there to prepare a place for you. And if I go and prepare a place for you, I will come back and take you to be with me that you also may be where I am."

Though a waiting mansion appealed to Stamphill and others who had experienced the poverty of the American depression in the 1930s, the picture according to the NIV that Jesus paints of a room in his Father's house is more intimate. God has a house. His house is large enough to have many inhabitants, all with enough room to have what they need, while, most importantly, living in the dwelling of the King himself. The Son invited his followers to live in his own house, the house he shares with his Father. Great picture, isn't it?

The thought before that in Scripture had to do with the dead inhabiting the world of the dead before the final judgment. For example, Jesus told a story about a rich man and a man named Lazarus who both died and went to an existence in that realm.

> The time came when the beggar died and the angels carried him to Abraham's side. The rich man also died and was buried. In hell, where he was in torment, he looked up and saw Abraham far away, with Lazarus by his side. So he called to him, "Father Abraham, have pity on me and send Lazarus to dip the tip of his finger in water and cool my tongue, because I am in agony in this fire." (Luke 16:22-24)

Yet as Jesus prepares himself to die, rise from the dead, and go back to the Father, the picture moves from the dead waiting either in Abraham's bosom or hell (hades) to after the judgment and to the ultimate promise of Jesus' followers living in the same realm as God himself.

If we take the reference to his preparing rooms for us to mean that all the saved will live in one dwelling, it seems we stretch the thought beyond its intent. Living in the next life isn't living all in the same house; it's all living in the presence of God.

That said, I still like the idea of Jesus preparing my dwelling, even if that is not meant so literally as him going home to do carpentry in anticipation of my arrival. Speaking of that, I cannot imagine a more appropriate occupation for the Creator of the earth and stars than carpentry. Is it possible that Jesus chose that line of work while he lived among us because of his passion for making things?

If the Master Creator—the Master Carpenter—tells me that he's preparing a dwelling place for me, he means it. My awe is not based on the concept that heaven is too good to be true. It's that my limited mind cannot harness enough imagination to anticipate what my new home will be like, a home prepared by the Master Creator. But I can use concepts from this life as a basic guideline to help me understand my heavenly home.

My very own dwelling in his Father's home.

God didn't leave us in the dark concerning heaven and the next life. We certainly don't know all of his plans, but we have more to go on than just speculation and guesswork. God provides previews of heaven in the Bible that can give us hope and anticipation to help us persevere when this life is difficult.

Perhaps as you read this book, your God-given imagination will allow you a glimpse into the world of eternity with the King of creativity.

Who Will Be in Heaven?

CNN recently aired an HBO special about the terrorist attack in Mumbai, India, that occurred November 26, 2008. Especially chilling was the captured telephone dialogue between the terrorists and their masters. Daniel Reed, the filmmaker, said, "Like me, many of the people I dealt with in the course of securing the astonishingly explicit footage and audio which I use in the film believed this was a story which needed to be told as accurately and faithfully as possible . . . ."

And he did.

Throughout the sordid affair, masters/controllers spoke via phone often with their men bringing death and destruction to as many people as possible. For example, in the audios you hear instructions to assassinate certain hostages, followed by gunfire, and then reports of completion.

If I had been asked ahead of time to guess the emotions demonstrated in those audios, I would have predicted high emotions, fear, anger, shouting, and such. I would have been wrong. Dead wrong. That's what makes the audio so terrifying. Not only the masters, but also the terrorists, talked calmly as they massacred people. As instructions came, the terrorists replied, praising their god before completing their assignments. When it looked as if some of the terrorists might be captured, the masters told them to kill themselves so that their god would be pleased and bring them to live with him. Before they shot themselves, or rushed into a hail of Indian bullets, they softly asked their god to accept their martyrdom.

In short, they had no doubt they were heaven bound.

Indignant, are you?

So am I, but it's not just them. From the way people talk about heaven, it would appear easier to discuss who will *not* be there than who will be there. It seems that unless a person is an agnostic, atheist, or holds some other philosophy that discounts life after this one, nearly everyone believes that he or she will be in heaven.

Good Old American Optimism

Throughout my life, I've encountered many who believe they are heaven bound but have no apparent understanding of godliness and righteousness. The other night I caught the end of a story on television about a recently retired pornography starlet. As the program concluded, the interviewer asked her friends if she were going to heaven when she died. They each replied in the affirmative, citing her goodness and genuine concern for people. Finally, they asked the starlet herself. She gave the same answer.

If you happened to see the same program and feel that I'm not being fair to the woman, please do not misunderstand. I'm not trying to judge the heart and soul of a person whom I don't know and have no idea where she is now in her own spiritual life. My intent is not to condemn a specific person, but to illustrate. My point is that a large number of people that typical churches would not consider saved believe that they are definitely headed for heaven when they leave this life. Are we all going? Porn stars? Religious zealots who murder? Universal salvation for us all?

I hate to be negative here, but we should examine the words of Jesus on the matter.

"Enter through the narrow gate. For wide is the gate and broad is the road that leads to destruction, and many enter through it. But small is the gate and narrow the road that leads to life, and only a few find it." (Matthew 7:13-14)

"Not everyone who says to me, 'Lord, Lord,' will enter the kingdom of heaven, but only he who does the will of my Father who is in heaven. Many will say to me on that day,'Lord, Lord, did we not prophesy in your name, and in your name drive out demons and perform many miracles?' Then I will tell them plainly, 'I never knew you. Away from me, you evil-doers!'" (Matthew 7:21-23)

Tough words, aren't they? Jesus said that the majority of people travel a road of destruction and only the minority find the road that leads to life. He went on to say there will be folks claiming that they worked for him, giving examples of their actions, but he will reply that he never knew them. You wouldn't think those folks would purposely lie to Jesus because they know that he knows everything. So perhaps they themselves believe that they served Jesus and will be shocked to hear him say, "I never knew you. Away from me, you evildoers."

In a world seeking tolerance, understanding, and mutual respect between nations, peoples, religions, and anything else you can think of, those words don't appear to fit. After all, there is Judaism, Islam, Buddhism, Christianity, and much more. Looking at the worldwide picture, it seems reasonable to conclude that a person's choice of religion results not so much from personal study and conviction but from tradition and cultural exposure.

This conclusion applies not just to the major religions but to subsets within those religions. I recall asking a famous Christian evangelist why he chose the denomination in which he served. He replied that the little Texas town he grew up in had two churches and that, "like most people, I went to the one that showed me the most love." That's not to say that he had no doctrinal or denominational convictions. It is to say that his exposure to both groups drew him to one over the other before he was old enough to have doctrinal or denominational convictions. If he had gone to the other church, he likely would have viewed some tenets of the Christian faith differently from the ones he was taught by the group he chose.

Does that matter?

Some Protestants are convinced that Catholics aren't Christians and some Catholics believe that Catholicism is the only true representation of Christianity. Within the broader Protestant spectrum, there are major disagreements between Calvinists and Arminians, between pre-rapture, post-rapture, and no-rapture eschatologists, and between immersers and sprinklers. The list goes on, of course, but you get the idea. The fact that there *were* two churches in that small Texas town indicates that each group saw some things differently from the other. And they likely viewed those differences as important enough to have two congregations, so that the Christians who were right wouldn't have to worship with the Christians who were wrong.

If someone chooses the "wrong" group because that group showed him more love, is he or she lost? Should he or she forget about heaven?

Every once in a while, just for the frustration of it, I surf the net to find Web sites posted by very small sects within Christianity that purport to be the only true believers, claiming that all the rest who think they are Christians will hear Jesus denouncing their so-called service to him come judgment day. This situation probably helps explain the bumper sticker that reads, "I like Jesus. It's his followers I can't stand."

Since I write as a Christian, you may think I'm being too hard on my own kind. Nah. I think the bumper sticker may have an insight into ourselves that we need.

What About This Jesus Guy?

Jesus did not hesitate to claim that he is God. He said in John 10:30, "I and the Father are one." He makes a bolder statement a few chapters later:

Jesus answered, "I am the way and the truth and the life. No one comes to the Father except through me. If you really knew me, you would know my Father as well. From now on, you do know him and have seen him."

Philip said, "Lord, show us the Father and that will be enough for us."

Jesus answered: "Don't you know me, Philip, even after I have been among you such a long time? Anyone who has seen me has seen the Father. How can you say, 'Show us the Father'? (John 14:6-9, NAS)

No one comes to the Father but through Jesus. That's the key. If anyone is to be with the Father, it will be because of Jesus. That holds true even for those who do not know Jesus, but are known by Jesus.

Should I say that more plainly? Some are saved through Jesus though they do not know who he is; they are saved because he knows them.

The Ones Who Lived Before Jesus

In his letter to the Romans, the Apostle Paul provides his theme early. It's in Romans 1:17: "the just shall live by faith." Similar words had been written many years earlier in Habakkuk 2:4 as part of a message of hope for the people of God under siege. For Paul this amazing truth—life with God is by faith—would serve as the basis for his continually affirmed message that salvation is by grace through faith, not by anything we can accomplish on our own.

> But because of his great love for us, God, who is rich in mercy, made us alive with Christ even when we were dead in transgressions—it is by grace you have been saved. And God raised us up with Christ and seated us with him in the heavenly realms in Christ Jesus, in order that in the coming ages he might show the incomparable riches of his grace, expressed in his kindness to us in Christ Jesus. For it is by grace you have been saved, through faith—and this not from yourselves, it is the gift of God— not by works, so that no one can boast. (Ephesians 2:4-9a)

After establishing the theme of living by faith early in Romans 1, Paul immediately rips into the sins of those who were not the people of God (Gentiles), followed by just as intense an attack on the sins of the people who were supposed to know God (Jews). He concludes that none of us is righteous (3:10). To emphasize his point to those who might wish to excuse themselves from this analysis, he jabs, "no, not one." All have fallen short of God's requirements; no one deserves heaven, neither Gentile nor Jew (3:23).

The good news is that he doesn't end there. He immediately writes that we can be

> . . . justified freely by his grace through the redemption that came by Christ Jesus. God presented him as a sacrifice of atonement, through faith in his blood. He did this to demonstrate his justice, because in his forbearance he had left the sins committed beforehand unpunished—he did it to demonstrate his justice at the present time, so as to be just and the one who justifies those who have faith in Jesus. (Romans 3:24-26)

This passage alone could take a book to discuss, but we concentrate here on one phrase: "because in his forbearance he had left the sins committed beforehand unpunished—he did it to demonstrate his justice . . . ." Those who lived before Jesus Christ would benefit from his atonement just as much as those who lived during his human journey and afterwards. The ones before didn't have faith in Jesus per se, because the Messiah had not yet come. However, they would be given eternal life just as those who lived in the time of Jesus and thereafter.

You may accept what I just said, but you may not accept what I'm about to say. The atonement accomplished by Jesus would cover those who were the people of God that we read about in the Old Testament. However, his atonement also gave eternal life to some people that the Jewish people of the Old Testament had no knowledge of. That's right, uncircumcised Gentiles. People who were not the physical descendants of Abraham. His atonement would provide salvation for some who didn't follow the Patriarchs and didn't follow the Law of Moses.

But I move too quickly. Before getting to that, let's make this atonement idea simpler to grasp.

The Fall

Let's start back at the beginning, at the creation of humankind in the Garden of Eden.

Life in the garden was idyllic in comparison to the experience we have on earth now. There were no diseases, no traffic jams, no in-laws, and not even a Congress to worry about. Just two people in a perfect garden having regular visits from the Father God who loved them.

Then it got *all* messed up.

God warned Adam and Eve that if they sinned, they would die: ". . . you must not eat from the tree of the knowledge of good and evil, for when you eat of it you will surely die" (Genesis 2:17). But Eve, then Adam, disobeyed God by eating the fruit of that forbidden tree: "When the woman saw that the fruit of the tree was good for food and pleasing to the eye, and also desirable for gaining wisdom, she took some and ate it. She also gave some to her husband, who was with her, and he ate it" (Genesis 3:6).

Just as he had forewarned, God took life from them. Living on this earth forever in their human bodies was no longer possible. God told them that they would die if they sinned, and death is what they received as recompense for their actions. Of humankind God decreed: "He must not be allowed to reach out his hand and take also from the tree of life and eat, and live forever" (Genesis 3:22).

By losing access to the Tree of Life, humans would now devolve to a different level of living, including dying—something that had not existed before sin occurred. "By the sweat of your brow you will eat your food until you return to the ground, since from it you were taken; for dust you are and to dust you will return" (Genesis 3:19).

As bad as that was, the penalty included more than physical death. It also meant separation from God, which is spiritual death. From that point, humankind would not only wish to find a way to live forever, by again benefiting from the Tree of Life, but would also crave a union with God that had been lost by unfaithfulness to the Father. Paul summed it up in Romans 6:23, "For the wages of sin is death, but the gift of God is eternal life in Christ Jesus our Lord." The goal of humanity is to regain eternal life in the presence of God, the very thing humans had at the beginning but so foolishly cast away. We didn't need saving in the beginning because Adam and Eve were not separated from the Father. They communed with him in the garden. He "walked" with them in the garden in the cool of the day (Genesis 3:8).

Jesus provides us a way to get back to the garden.

The Dilemma

Human sin created a sort of divine dilemma for God. He did not cease loving humankind, but he would enforce his law. As we've seen, the law of God said that sin brings death. It was stated in the garden, repeated in passages such as Ezekiel 18:20, and proclaimed by Paul in Romans 6:23. Humankind (Adam and Eve) sinned and as a result brought upon themselves death and separation from God. They reaped what they sowed. That would have been the end of the story except for the fact that God refused to quit loving or to abandon these creatures he had made.

How could God uphold his word while at the same time redeeming humankind from the consequences of sin?

That was the dilemma.

The solution would be to have every sin punished by death, but not necessarily by the death of the specific person who committed the sin. Doesn't sound right, does it? We know from passages such as Ezekiel 18:20 that we bear responsibility for our own sins, not the sins of those around us. "The soul who sins is the one who will die. The son will not share the guilt of the father, nor will the father share the guilt of the son. The righteousness of the righteous man will be credited to him, and the wickedness of the wicked will be charged against him."

No human being could take my place because each of us stands guilty of our own sinfulness. However, God could fulfill the demands of his law by taking the punishment on himself. That's what he chose to do. The Son would stand in place of the sinner. He would die, not just physically, but also in a temporary separation from the Father as he was "made sin" for us on the cross. Paul explained it this way: "God made him who had no sin to be sin for us, so that in him we might become the righteousness of God" (2 Corinthians 5:21).

The Second Adam

To atone for the actions of the first Adam in the garden, the second Adam, Jesus Christ, would take the punishment for every sin from the first all the way to the end of this world. With that in mind, read carefully and slowly:

> Therefore, just as sin entered the world through one man, and death through sin, and in this way death came to all men, because all sinned . . . death reigned from the time of Adam to the time of Moses, even over those who did not sin by breaking a command, as did Adam, who was a pattern of the one to come. But the gift is not like the trespass. For if the many died by the trespass of the one man, how much more did God's grace and the gift that came by the grace of the one man, Jesus Christ, overflow to the many! Again, the gift of God is not like the result of the one man's sin: The judgment followed one sin and brought condemnation, but the gift followed many trespasses and brought justification. For if, by the trespass of the one man, death reigned through that one man, how much more will those who receive God's abundant provision of grace and of the gift of righteousness reign in life through the one man, Jesus Christ. Consequently, just as the result of one

trespass was condemnation for all men, so also the result of one act of righteousness was justification that brings life for all men. For just as through the disobedience of the one man the many were made sinners, so also through the obedience of the one man the many will be made righteous. (Romans 5:12-19)

Jesus took our places—if we accept such a gift—so that two things can occur: 1. We can live with God. 2. We can live forever. We are re-united with God to have what Adam and Eve enjoyed with him. We also get transformed bodies that will have access to the Tree of Life and, therefore, live forever.

As you will see as we progress through this book, living forever also means living here, on a New Earth, in its pristine condition as it was before sin and death marred perfection. We won't live as spooks, ghosts, or spirits, but in bodies as God originally intended. Yes, real bodies, but bodies not corrupted by the consequences of sin in the garden.

What About Those Folks Mentioned Earlier?

I enjoy being a Bible student, though my training left me short of becoming a Bible scholar. I see my job as asking questions rather than presuming that I should have all the answers. Maybe the intellectuals can figure out some of the answers and assist us; meanwhile the rest of us can try our best to live according to God's grace as we continue to read and study the Scriptures.

Freed from the need to defend an entrenched doctrinal position or to placate denominational leaders focused on maintaining their doctrinal paradigm, I merrily dig into the verses that seemingly do not fit things I've previously been taught. A rebel? I don't see myself as such. I have no desire to upset the status quo; I just don't always accept it.

Now that I've confessed, let's examine the idea that some will be in heaven because of Jesus' atonement who have not committed themselves to the same Jesus that I believe to be the Son of God.

Several years ago I had the thrill of teaching Old Testament Survey to freshmen at a Christian college. The first day of class, I gave a pop quiz of one hundred questions to discover how much these fine young people from solid churches and solid families knew about the Old Testament. Most questions were left completely blank. The average number of answers was six. The average number of correct answers was three. One guy wrote on his otherwise blank paper, "That's what I'm here for!"

I hope you know more about the Old Testament than my students in that class. If so, you won't be surprised by the story that looms large when thinking of our subject. It begins in Numbers 22. The protagonist's name is Balaam.

We don't have the space to discuss Balaam in detail. You can find his story in Numbers 22-24, Numbers 26:8-16, Deuteronomy 23:4, and a very unflattering reference to him in Revelation 2:14. The summary goes like this:

The Israelites were coming toward the land of Moab after soundly defeating the Amorites. Moab's king, Balak, sent for a prophet of

God named Balaam. He paid Balaam to ask God to curse the Israelites heading into the territory. Balaam didn't know who these people were but went to God with the deal. God refused. The king offered more money. Balaam went back to God with the better offer and was nearly killed for his greediness. (Remember the story of the Angel of Jehovah and the talking donkey?) Later Balaam would help the Israelites' enemies find ways to thwart the Jews and God would punish him for it. Balaam turned out to be a bad guy and we learn about what happens when people do bad things.

However, that's not what interests us here.

Did you note that Balaam was a prophet of God who had never heard of the Israelites? He wasn't a Jew. He wasn't a descendant of Abraham. How in the world could Balaam be an uncircumcised Gentile in the service of Almighty God, when Jehovah had made clear all the way back in Genesis 17 that he had chosen the descendants of Abraham to be his people? There is no indication that Balaam was circumcised, kept the holy days or feasts, or showed any other indication of being one of God's people. Yet, there he is. One of God's prophets. The Lord himself speaks with Balaam.

I have no great theological point to make here concerning Balaam, circumcision, or donkeys. Not even greed. My intent is to show that often when we think we know all about the rules and ways of God, he throws us a zinger that doesn't fit what we think we know. There is no doubt that Abraham's descendants were God's people, that they looked for a coming Messiah, that the males were to be circumcised, that they were to keep holy days, tithe, and a host of other things. If we were living with the Jews in that day, every one of those things would be required of us.

But apparently not Balaam.

The later references to Balaam in the Bible indicate that we shouldn't waste time looking around heaven and the New Earth for him. He went from being a prophet of God to receiving the wrath of God. Nevertheless, that's not my point. The point is that before Balaam did the bad stuff, he was a prophet of God. He had a relationship with God that doesn't fit the rules that we think we understand.

It seems that God does not feel compelled to explain everything to our satisfaction.

Good for God. Personally, I don't know how awed I would be by a God that I could completely understand and explain.

But Balaam's story is not the only one that throws a wrench into the works. You may find it interesting to read through this text:

> This Melchizedek was king of Salem and priest of God Most High. He met Abraham returning from the defeat of the kings and blessed him, and Abraham gave him a tenth of everything. First, his name means "king of righteousness"; then also, "king of Salem" means "king of peace." Without father or mother, without genealogy, without beginning of days or end of life, like the Son of God he remains a priest forever. Just think how great he was: Even the patriarch Abraham gave him a tenth of the plunder!

Now the law requires the descendants of Levi who become priests to collect a tenth from the people—that is, their brothers—even though their brothers are descended from Abraham. This man, however, did not trace his descent from Levi, yet he collected a tenth from Abraham and blessed him who had the promises. (Hebrews 7:1-6)

Melchizedek was not a patriarch, at least not one that we have knowledge of. Not related to Abraham. Yet a priest of God. He appears from nowhere (as far as the story goes) and then disappears again. The Hebrew writer uses him as an analogy to the priesthood of Jesus himself because Jewish understanding would preclude Jesus being a priest because he was not a descendant of Levi. Well, neither was good old Melchizedek. Yet Abraham himself paid a tithe to him. Melchizedek was a great priest of God, and so is the descendant of Judah named Jesus bar Joseph (Jesus the Son of Joseph).

This guy doesn't fit the pattern. We don't know much about him. However, I expect to see Melchizedek in heaven. Apparently the Hebrew writer does as well.

How About a New Testament Example?

If Old Testament stories don't make you scratch your head and conclude that God cannot be put in a box, maybe this New Testament passage will:

All who sin apart from the law will also perish apart from the law, and all who sin under the law will be judged by the law. For it is not those who hear the law who are righteous in God's sight, but it is those who obey the law who will be declared righteous. (Indeed, when Gentiles, who do not have the law, do by nature things required by the law, they are a law for themselves, even though they do not have the law, since they show that the requirements of the law are written on their hearts, their consciences also bearing witness, and their thoughts now accusing, now even defending them.) This will take place on the day when God will judge men's secrets through Jesus Christ, as my gospel declares. (Romans 2:12-16)

In the above passage, Paul is midstride in chastising the Jewish people of his day for condemning Gentiles' sins while sinning themselves. "You, therefore, have no excuse, you who pass judgment on someone else, for at whatever point you judge the other, you are condemning yourself, because you who pass judgment do the same things" (Romans 2:1).

Rather than admitting comparable behavior, they found comfort in having the law (of Moses) that the Gentiles did not have. To their way of thinking, Gentiles were obviously wicked people because they didn't have the blessed law given to the Jews. Therefore, Gentiles sins are bad, Jewish sins are not as bad—or something like that.

Paul makes short work of that view.

He says that it's not *having* the law that matters; it's *obeying* the law. Then he tosses a grenade. He unexpectedly asserts that Gentiles who do by nature things required by the law become a law to themselves. Furthermore, the law of their hearts is attested to by their own consciences.

It doesn't seem likely that doing by nature the "things required by the law" includes circumcision, observing holy days, making animal sacrifices, and the like. It appears beyond imagination that some guy wakes up one morning and tells his wife, "I'm not sure why, but I believe I'm supposed to circumcise myself." The law of the heart ties to the greatest commandments rather than to a prescribed ritual. Consider these passages as one thought:

> "'Love the Lord your God with all your heart and with all your soul and with all your mind.' This is the first and greatest commandment. And the second is like it: 'Love your neighbor as yourself.' All the Law and the Prophets hang on these two commandments." (Matthew 22:37-38)

> The commandments, "Do not commit adultery," "Do not murder," "Do not steal," "Do not covet," and whatever other commandment there may be, are summed up in this one rule: "Love your neighbor as yourself." (Romans 13:9)

What does Paul say is the fate of those who obey the law of the heart? In reference to their consciences' defending them, he writes,

"This will take place on the day when God will judge men's secrets through Jesus Christ, as my gospel declares." As those under the Old Testament would be forgiven by the work of Jesus the Christ, so would the Gentiles who yielded to the law of the heart. Of course, they didn't obey the law of the heart perfectly, just as no one (except Jesus) obeyed the Law of Moses perfectly. We all sin. We are all imperfect. None earns his salvation. God saves us through Jesus based on his atonement, not our meticulous obedience. Paul lets the Jews know that they aren't saved by their perfect obedience to the law. Gentiles aren't saved by perfect obedience to the law of the heart. Salvation is by grace through faith. Yet, at least in the case of the Gentiles referred to here, they didn't know how to place their faith in a Christ they had never heard of. But by his grace, God chose to view their seeking to follow the law of the heart as a sign of their faith in him. They hadn't rejected Jesus; they didn't know of Jesus. Therefore, based on the intent of their hearts, God gave grace to all those who lived before Jesus and sought to do right, whether they had the Law of Moses or not.

Does That Work Now?

Maybe you're thinking, "Wait a minute. Are you claiming that people in our day will be saved though they don't follow Jesus as I believe they should?" In response, I refer to the words of Jesus quoted earlier. It is not those who claim they know him who will taste heaven. It is those whom *he* knows.

Except for Christian sects that reject anyone else's salvation but their own, most Christians believe that people with many different understandings of doctrine will be in heaven—all of whom are saved by the atonement of Jesus. Calvinists and Arminians. Those who believe in congregational self-government, those who believe in presbyterian or espiscopal government. Those who believe in free will, those who embrace the bondage of the will. Those who like contemporary worship, those who like their hymn writers long dead. Those who use the King James Version only; those who don't have a clue how to understand the language of the KJV. The list goes on, but you get the idea. Our differences of understanding might keep us from worshipping together as part of one body of believers here, but they won't there. (It shouldn't here either, but that is another study for another time. John 17:20-21)

As an old Southern Gospel song used to tell it, it's not what name is over the door of your church that determines whether you will be in heaven; it's what's in your heart. God hasn't ever saved one person who understood it all correctly and obeyed perfectly. Not one. He chooses to save those who live by love, and he does it through the atonement of Jesus.

Admittedly, I take it a step further than many Christians.

Just as there were priests in the Bible who don't fit what we know of God's laws, prophets who never heard of the chosen people, and Gentiles who were saved not by following the law of Moses but because of their hearts, I believe there are those outside our paradigm today who are known by Jesus though they may not be known by the church. The fact that followers of Jesus exclude them doesn't affect how God sees them. For example, John apparently felt the same way about a person who was not a recognizable part of their group. "Teacher," said John, "we saw a man driving out demons in your name and we told him to stop, because he was not one of us." "Do not stop him," Jesus said. "No one who does a miracle in my name can in the next moment say anything bad about me, for whoever is not against us is for us" (Mark 9:38-40).

But Those Without Faith in Jesus?

There is no doubt that salvation is by grace through faith. I teach as many as I can about Jesus and urge them to place their faith in him. I call them to repentance and godly living. That hasn't changed and never will. In the truest sense of the word, my heart is the heart of an evangelist.

However, a person claiming faith in Jesus who selfishly lives discordantly with the law of the heart isn't at the top of the list of those I expect to share heaven with. On the other hand, I anticipate seeing people there who lived by faith—though they weren't sure exactly whom to place that faith in—and who had a heart that directed them to kindness and love for others. Sinners all, you understand, but sinners forgiven by the grace of God through the atonement of Jesus.

As Peter preached on Pentecost, "The promise is for you and your children and for all who are far off—for all whom the Lord our God will call" (Acts 2:39).

God makes the call.

It is by grace through faith that we are saved, and that not of ourselves. Jesus saves. I'm happy to leave that to him, though his choices don't always coincide with the choices of churches of which I have been a part. These are the kind of people Paul says God saves:

> Neither the sexually immoral nor idolaters nor adulterers nor male prostitutes nor homosexual offenders nor thieves nor the greedy nor drunkards nor slanderers nor swindlers will inherit the kingdom of God. And that is what some of you were. *But you were washed, you were sanctified, you were justified in the name of the Lord Jesus Christ and by the Spirit of our God.* (1 Corinthians 6:9-11, emphasis mine)

To conclude, not everyone will be in heaven, but everyone in heaven will be a sinner who has been forgiven. Forgiveness comes through the atonement of Jesus. He knows those who are his, and it isn't always the people who think they are (remember Matthew 7.) I place my faith in Jesus and urge you to do the same. Anyone he chooses to save is my brother or sister and I will be honored to share heaven with them.

If you fear that you wouldn't like heaven because Jesus may save some folks you don't think should be there, perhaps you should consider another home for eternity.

What Will We Be in Heaven?

"Heaven will be vastly different from this life."

I'm sure you've heard that said many times. On occasion I've imagined my existence in the eternal as being anything from universal exploration (similar to the ending of *2001: A Space Odyssey*) to being absent of free will or a single independent thought (singing forever in harmony with all the rest in an eternal church service).

One of the reasons my imagination entertains scenarios of the New Earth I will one day experience is because I have only experienced this one; it is natural to imagine what comes next. However, what fuels my curiosity as much as the promise of heaven is the future condition of something with which I am very familiar—me. What will I be like in heaven? Will I still have *my* memories, *my* emotions, and *my* personality? Will I still have those unique qualities that make me, *me*? Or will death strip me entirely of my personal identity and idiosyncrasies?

What Are Human Beings?

To determine if human beings will be different in the next life, we must first understand what it means to be human.

We are a unique bunch. Based on what the Bible tells us, humans were the last beings God created. It wasn't just that God created us after he made the animals on earth; God created us after he created the heavenly beings we call angels. We were created to have a different role and place in the universe than any other creature.

If you have read any of my previous books, you may recall references to the triune nature of humans. We consist of three inseparable components. We are *body*, meaning we are physical bodies of flesh and blood (Hebrews 2:14); we are *mind*, meaning we are both intellectual and emotional (Mark 5:15); and we are *spirit*, meaning there is a part of us that is different from the physical and exists to commune with God (Zechariah 12:1, Ecclesiastes 12:7).

A human is not complete without all three. God and the angels are essentially spirits, though they are capable of inhabiting human bodies and even animals, according to the Bible (John 4:24, Hebrews 1:14). Consider a few examples:

1   Angels appeared as men to Abraham and Lot (Genesis 18-19).

2   Angels can appear as or with horses or chariots of fire (2 Kings 2:11; 6:17).

3 An angel who looked like a "young man" told Mary
    Magdalene, Mary the mother of Jesus, and Salome that
    Jesus had risen from the dead (Mark 16:5-7).

4 Hebrews 13:2 tells us not to "forget to entertain strangers,
    for by doing so, some people have entertained angels
    without knowing it." (For further study on angels and
    spiritual beings, see my book, *Seeing the Unseen*.)

One difference from God and angels is that we humans are spiritual *and* physical. It's not that we are spirits who happen to inhabit a body or a body waiting for a spirit, but by our very nature, we are spirit and body.

Concerning our existence in heaven it therefore seems logical to ask: "Will we still be human?" When God raises us from the dead, will we become something other than human? Will we become another species? A different life form entirely?

Resurrection Bodies

When Jesus died, God raised him from the dead with a new kind of body, and when he ascended into heaven, he remained in that body. Do you remember some of the things Jesus did in his resurrection body?

Jesus walked, talked, and even ate food while in his resurrected body.

Jesus said to them, "Come and have breakfast." None of the disciples dared ask him, "Who are you?" They knew it was the Lord. Jesus came, took the bread and gave it to them, and did the same with the fish. This was now the third time Jesus appeared to his disciples after he was raised from the dead. (John 21:12-14)

And while they still did not believe it because of joy and amazement, he asked them, "Do you have anything here to eat?" They gave him a piece of broiled fish, and he took it and ate it in their presence. (Luke 24:41-43)

To calm the disciples during a post-resurrection appearance, Jesus pointedly told them that he was in an actual body and not some sort of disembodied spirit.

Jesus himself stood among them and said to them, "Peace be with you."

They were startled and frightened, thinking they saw a ghost. He said to them, "Why are you troubled, and why do doubts rise in your minds? Look at my hands and my feet. It is I myself! Touch me and see; a ghost does not have flesh and bones, as you see I have."

When he had said this, he showed them his hands and feet. (Luke 24:36-40)

A week later his disciples were in the house again, and Thomas was with them. Though the doors were locked, Jesus came and stood among them and said, "Peace be with you!" Then he said to Thomas, "Put your finger here; see my hands. Reach out your hand and put it into my side. Stop doubting and believe."

Thomas said to him, "My Lord and my God!" (John 20:26-28)

When Jesus didn't want to be recognized by those who knew him well, he changed his appearance.

As they approached the village to which they were going, Jesus acted as if he were going farther. But they urged him strongly, "Stay with us, for it is nearly evening; the day is almost over." So he went in to stay with them.

When he was at the table with them, he took bread, gave thanks, broke it and began to give it to them. Then their eyes were opened and they recognized him, and he disappeared from their sight. They asked each other, "Were not our hearts burning within us while he talked with us on the road and opened the Scriptures to us?"

They got up and returned at once to Jerusalem. There they found the Eleven and those with them, assembled together and saying, "It is true! The Lord has risen and has appeared to Simon." Then the two told what had happened on the way, and how Jesus was recognized by them when he broke the bread. (Luke 24:28-35)

They could touch him as well as see him, but this body was amazing. He could change appearance in his resurrected body, suddenly appear in a locked room startling people, disappear from dinner with another group, and do other extraordinary things that humans cannot do. However, he also did things that humans do in their physical bodies. The resurrected body, as astonishing as it was, also enjoyed eating and apparently had the ability to digest the food.

Several passages tell us that our resurrected bodies will be like Jesus' resurrected body:

If only for this life we have hope in Christ, we are to be pitied more than all men. But Christ has indeed been raised from the dead, the firstfruits of those who have fallen asleep. For since death came through a man, the resurrection of the dead comes also through a man. For as in Adam all die, so in Christ all will be made alive. (1 Corinthians 15:19-22)

So will it be with the resurrection of the dead. The body that is sown is perishable, it is raised imperishable; it is sown in dishonor, it is raised in glory; it is sown in weakness, it is raised in power; it is sown a natural body, it is raised a spiritual body.

If there is a natural body, there is also a spiritual body. So it is written: "The first man Adam became a living being"; the last Adam, a life-giving spirit. The spiritual did not come first, but the natural, and after that the spiritual. The first man was of the dust of the earth, the second man from heaven. As was the earthly man, so are those who are of the earth; and as is the man from heaven, so also are those who are of heaven. And just as we have borne the likeness of the earthly man, so shall we bear the likeness of the man from heaven. (1 Corinthians 15:42-49)

But our citizenship is in heaven. And we eagerly await a Savior from there, the Lord Jesus Christ, who, by the power that enables him to bring everything under his control, will transform our lowly bodies so that they will be like his glorious body. (Philippians 3:20-21)

Dear friends, now we are children of God, and what we will be has not yet been made known. But we know that when he appears, we shall be like him, for we shall see him as he is. (1 John 3:2)

Jesus was the first to experience resurrection from the dead and to walk around in the body that will last forever. Others in the Bible had been brought back to life, but not in the same way that Jesus was resurrected. For example, Lazarus came back to the very same body that he had before death, a body that would, therefore, die again (John 11:44). Lazarus' body was still limited by all that is fallen humanity. But the body that Jesus came back to earth with will never die again.

Jesus' resurrection body was superior to the body we inherited from Adam's sin. That is why Paul referred to Jesus as the first fruits of the resurrection. He is the second Adam in that he was the first to inhabit the glorious (as Paul called it in Philippians) resurrection body. The wonderful news, according to Paul, is that we as God's children, like Jesus, will receive new bodies when we are resurrected: "We know that the whole creation has been groaning as in the pains of childbirth right up to the present time. Not only so, but we ourselves, who have the first fruits of the Spirit, groan inwardly as we wait eagerly for our adoption as sons, the redemption of our bodies" (Romans 8:22-23).

We groan for the redemption of our bodies. Though we already have the first fruits of the Spirit, which is the indwelling of God's Holy Spirit within us, we long for the glorified body to make us complete. Jesus possessed the Spirit before his resurrection and received the glorified body when he rose from the grave. We can experience the same because of God's indescribable grace.

Our Current Bodies

Paul calls our present bodies seeds for our resurrection bodies. God will use these bodies to form our resurrection bodies, just as a farmer uses a seed to grow a plant.

> But someone may ask, "How are the dead raised? With what kind of body will they come?" How foolish! What you sow does not come to life unless it dies. When you sow, you do not plant the body that will be, but just a seed, perhaps of wheat or of something else. But God gives it a body as he has determined,

and to each kind of seed he gives its own body. All flesh is not the same: Men have one kind of flesh, animals have another, birds another and fish another. (1 Corinthians 15:35-39)

Just as we wouldn't expect a carrot seed to grow a stalk of corn, we wouldn't expect a human seed to become another species such as an angel. In this case a human seed will become a glorified, spirit-filled human in an ageless body that lasts forever—similar to Adam's body before God took away access to the Tree of Life. A better human body for sure, but a human body nonetheless. Paul goes on:

There are also heavenly bodies and there are earthly bodies; but the splendor of the heavenly bodies is one kind, and the splendor of the earthly bodies is another. The sun has one kind of splendor, the moon another and the stars another; and star differs from star in splendor.

So will it be with the resurrection of the dead. The body that is sown is perishable, it is raised imperishable; it is sown in dishonor, it is raised in glory; it is sown in weakness, it is raised in power; it is sown a natural body, it is raised a spiritual body. If there is a natural body, there is also a spiritual body. (1 Corinthians 15:40-44)

Notice that Paul says "a spiritual body." It is important to note that he does *not* say a bodiless spirit. Paul is clear that it is not *this* exact body that will be resurrected: "I declare to you, brothers, that flesh and blood cannot inherit the kingdom of God, nor does the perishable inherit the imperishable" (1 Corinthians 15:50).

However, he is just as clear that it is a body. From the passages cited thus far in this chapter, we know it will be like Jesus' resurrection body, which means it will no longer be the perishable flesh and blood that we are now. It will be different in some ways. Similar in others. In that body I expect to eat as did Jesus in his resurrected body, but I will have an incorruptible body that will not age or die.

Personally, I like that combination. (Grow those tomatoes, Shank, I'm coming to have some. . . .)

Can a Resurrection Body Remember the Former Life?

In his resurrected body—the body the Bible tells us is like the body we will receive—Jesus remembered what had happened before his natural body died. He maintained his memories and knowledge, including his friends and his mission. He still knew how to get to the meeting place of his disciples. He was still himself, though in a wonderful new body. He had not lost his identity. Other humans could still recognize him, though they did not always recognize him right away, but absolutely could when he was ready for them to know who he was.

It seems reasonable to assume that Jesus' resurrection body remained ethnically Jewish. There is no indication that he was treated as a Gentile or Samaritan. Passages such as Revelation 7:9 imply that our own resurrection bodies will maintain certain racial traits: "After this I looked, and there before me was a great multitude that no one could count, from every nation, tribe, people and language, standing before the throne and in front of the Lamb."

Will We Recognize Each Other?

We will recognize each other in the next life as the disciples recognized Jesus. If you think about it, every reference to a specific person who had passed out of this world refers to that person by name, with his or her identity intact. For example, in the story of the Rich Man and Lazarus, Jesus portrayed both men as recognizing each other. Abraham actually says to the dead rich man; "Son, remember that in your lifetime you received your good things, while Lazarus received bad things, but now he is comforted here and you are in agony" (Luke 16:25). He said that the dead man could remember not only who he was, but what had transpired in his life. The rich man's final request gives evidence that he remembered his former life in detail: "Then I beg you, father, send Lazarus to my father's house, for I have five brothers. Let him warn them, so that they will not also come to this place of torment" (Luke 16:27-28).

Moses and Elijah came from the dead to see Jesus and to discuss Jesus' mission with him. The disciples present recognized Moses and Elijah, even though the text does not indicate that Jesus revealed their identities, and the disciples couldn't have known what Moses and Elijah looked like. The key here, though, is that both Moses and Elijah were *still* Moses and Elijah. Not only were they themselves, they knew what Jesus was about to face and had come to discuss it with him.

Two men, Moses and Elijah, appeared in glorious splendor, talking with Jesus. They spoke about his departure, which he was about to bring to fulfillment at Jerusalem. Peter and his companions were very sleepy, but when they became fully awake, they saw his glory and the two men standing with him. As the men were leaving Jesus, Peter said to him, "Master, it is good for us to be here. Let us put up three shelters—one for you, one for Moses and one for Elijah." (Luke 9:30-33)

Let's now look at this question from a slightly different angle.

Three Dimensions of Memory

If you were to study what scientists have learned about memory in humans, you'd find that they divide it into three categories. The first is sensory memory or sensory register. It is where information gathered by our five senses goes in its unprocessed form. For example, the ability to remember something you glimpsed only for a moment is sensory memory. It doesn't last long unless it is processed. A few minutes after seeing a new phone number, you likely don't remember it.

The second is short-term memory or working memory. It is, as its name says, short. It's sort of a scratch pad or desktop that you use to keep something in mind until you either dismiss it or transfer it to long-term memory. Back to our illustration of a phone number: if I just glance at it I may remember it briefly from sensory memory. If I repeat it to myself a couple of times so that I can immediately dial it, I'm using short-term memory. But unless I transfer the number to long-term memory, I don't remember it for long and have to look it up again if needed.

Unlike the first two types of memory, long-term memory has little decay. As the name states, it lasts longer than a few seconds or minutes. It is the place of memory storage. (Bored yet? Just wait; it gets very interesting in a moment.)

Long-term memory has two dimensions, declarative and procedural. Procedural memory is skill based. It's why you can still ride a bicycle even though you haven't been on one in years. It's why you don't have to learn to walk, drive, read, or write all over again every day.

Okay, now the interesting part: declarative memory. Declarative memory has two subsets, semantic and episodic. Semantic memory is a structured record of facts, concepts, and skills that we have acquired. It is why a person with amnesia can still know Sunday is the first day of the week, or that you go on the green light and stop at the red light. Episodic memory is the memory of events, experiences, and other dimensions of our lives that allow us to know who we are, where we came from, who we love, and the like. It is our autobiographical memory. From it we can tell stories of our childhood, remember our best friend in high school, and narrate all those other things that make us uniquely ourselves.

Those with retrograde amnesia lose some or all of episodic memory. They can still read or drive a car, but they don't know who they are or where they live.

If you're thinking, "What in the world does this have to do with heaven?" allow me to explain. Our episodic memory—events, people, and the like—is what makes us an individual who can function as a mature human being. Lose it and you don't know who you are, where you've been, or who you know. However, it is this very type of memory that some believe will be eliminated the moment we die. Repeatedly I have heard people say, "We won't have any memory of our lives here on earth after we die. If we did, we'd know which of our loved ones didn't make it to heaven and that would be too painful." In short, they believe that death brings about retrograde amnesia and that we all start over establishing a new autobiography, a new identity.

While I understand the fear some have of realizing someone they love isn't in heaven, the concept of having no memory to prevent that pain has no biblical basis. Every reference in Scripture to those who have died indicates that they still had their identity, their memories, and their unique individuality. Abraham is still Abraham, Moses still Moses, Elijah still Elijah, and so forth.

We will be able to recognize each other in heaven. We will know our family members, friends, and perhaps even some people we thought of as enemies.

Our new bodies will maintain our memories, emotions, and impressions of this world. I'm often stunned when people speculate that we will have no memories of this life in the next. In their minds, God will remove our memories and leave us in an eternal zombie-like state in which we don't even know who we were, much less who we are.

Our God is not out of touch with his creation. He made us as unique individuals and will not take that identity from us. The Bible tells us we are to store up for ourselves "treasures in heaven, where neither moth nor rust consumes and where thieves do not break in and steal" (Matthew 6:20 NRSV). In fact, God created humans to remember, feel, and think. It was his idea to begin with and when God created Adam and Eve with human traits, he called the creation "good." God will restore, not remove, what is good.

Your memories will not be stolen, erased, or deleted. God loves us just the way he created us and with him in charge, it's okay to be you. You will be loved and accepted as the person who has been molded in large part by your experiences. You will remember this first life and the lessons learned from it and will be all the more grateful for the return to what God called "good."

What About Scars or Body Defects?

After his resurrection Jesus showed the disciples the nail scars in his hands. Somehow the scars remained, even though the Holy Spirit resurrected him (Romans 8:11) with a new and wonderful resurrection body. Perhaps the scars were made to appear in the same way that he could alter his visage in that body; perhaps they were used as a means to help others recognize him. They served as a mark or a branding of sorts so that the disciples would know that his resurrection wasn't a ruse. Maybe the scars were there as symbols of his love, an honor lifting him up forever as the pinnacle of love.

Sometimes I wonder if our resurrection bodies will also have traits by which others will recognize us. Scars, birthmarks, and other things that may seem undesirable to us now might have different values and meanings in the next life. The beauty of the scars on the hands of Jesus was not the ugliness of the scars themselves; it was the reminder of Jesus' love and sacrifice for us.

In heaven on the New Earth, we might see the scars of those who were martyred as something beautiful, rather than unsightly. If they exist, it's possible that such markings won't be imperfections in the body but rather a spiritual symbol of glory and honor.

Let me be very clear that I am *not* saying that those who are deformed or have health problems will take those burdens to heaven with them. Paul referred to this body as a temporary dwelling in which we groan and are burdened. We don't wish simply to be free of this flawed body, he asserts, but to be in the new heavenly dwelling. This body is a tent, if you will; that body is a heavenly house. The problems of mortality—sickness, disease, disabilities, flaws, and the like—fold away with the earthly tent (body) and are replaced by one with no such problems.

Now we know that if the earthly tent we live in is destroyed, we have a building from God, an eternal house in heaven, not built by human hands. Meanwhile we groan, longing to be clothed with our heavenly dwelling, because when we are clothed, we will not be found naked. For while we are in this

tent, we groan and are burdened, because we do not wish
to be unclothed but to be clothed with our heavenly dwelling, so that what is mortal may be swallowed up by life. (2
Corinthians 5:1-4)

So will it be with the resurrection of the dead. The body that is
sown is perishable, it is raised imperishable; it is sown in dishonor, it is raised in glory; it is sown in weakness, it is raised
in power; (1 Corinthians 15:42-4)

Disabilities and deformities will *not* exist in heaven, though I believe
that some signs of honor for sufferings in this life could be evident.

Supernatural Abilities of the Resurrection Body

Earlier we mentioned that Jesus' resurrection body did things that
our human bodies cannot do. He could appear in a room with locked
doors, as he did to enter the room where his disciples were meeting
(John 20:19), and disappear into thin air as he did at Emmaus (Luke
24:31). Though his body was physical, it could operate differently from
our current physical bodies. Its ability was supernatural (considering
our current bodies to be natural).

It could be that Jesus had the ability to overcome the natural
simply because he was God. Our resurrection bodies might not have
those abilities. Nevertheless, the high-powered body we will receive
will no longer be suppressed by sin's curse and will, therefore, be able
to perform at its peak.

Human bodies in the Garden of Eden were superior to our current ones as well. Not only did those physical bodies live forever, but they never even got sick. Because of the emergence of sin, both of those traits were lost. Our new bodies, unaffected by the sin that led to the failure of these bodies, will have physical and spiritual abilities far above current levels.

What Age Will Our New Bodies Be?

As far as we know, God created Adam and Eve as fully grown, fully developed humans. They were adults at their full potential, the finished human product. That makes sense because they were created, not procreated. When humans reproduce, we procreate another human, but as we all know that baby has to be nurtured through infancy, childhood, and adolescence into adulthood. In the United States we typically don't consider children mentally mature enough to be on their own until they reach age eighteen.

If you have moved past your adolescence into mature adulthood, you likely discovered that at some point our bodies begin to deteriorate. We start small, grow to maturity, and then, at least in the case of most of the elderly I encounter, we start to shrink. We usually don't get back to our original weight (mine was 8 pounds 6 ounces), but we become physically weaker, and sometimes mentally weaker as well.

Basing my view on the way Adam and Eve functioned in the Garden of Eden, I do not believe that we will be young or old in our resurrection body. Aging didn't begin to matter until humankind lost contact with the Tree of Life. Our resurrection bodies will be in their fully developed state and eternally at their full potential. Our bodies will remain at full potential without any negative effects of aging because God provides access to the Tree and the River of Life in heaven.

Then the angel showed me the river of the water of life, as clear as crystal, flowing from the throne of God and of the Lamb down the middle of the great street of the city. On each side of the river stood the tree of life, bearing twelve crops of fruit, yielding its fruit every month. And the leaves of the tree are for the healing of the nations. No longer will there be any curse. The throne of God and of the Lamb will be in the city, and his servants will serve him. (Revelation 22:1-3)

If you recall, God removed the Tree of Life after Adam and Eve sinned. Without access to that amazing tree, human bodies can't stand the test of time, but when God restores what is good, he will restore our rights to eat the food from that tree and our bodies will have ceaseless life without arthritis, wheel chairs, false teeth, glasses, or nursing homes.

Will We Become Angels?

Clarence Oddbody worked diligently as George Bailey's guardian angel in the classic Christmas movie, "It's a Wonderful Life." You may remember that Clarence used to be a human being but became an angel after he died. He temporarily left heaven to "earn his wings" by showing George what life would've been like if he never existed.

Many movies portray people becoming angels after they die. I'm sure that the movie, "It's a Wonderful Life," did not intend to make theological statements; still, the entertainment industry has contributed to the common misconception that we cease to be humans after death and instead become angels.

Hebrews 2:5-17 explains that humans and angels are two very different types of beings:

It is not to angels that he has subjected the world to come, about which we are speaking. But there is a place where someone has testified: "What is man that you are mindful of him, the son of man that you care for him? You made him a little lower than the angels; you crowned him with glory and honor and put everything under his feet."

In putting everything under him, God left nothing that is not subject to him. Yet at present we do not see everything subject to him. But we see Jesus, who was made a little lower than the angels, now crowned with glory and honor because he suffered death, so that by the grace of God he might taste death for everyone.

In bringing many sons to glory, it was fitting that God, for whom and through whom everything exists, should make the author of their salvation perfect through suffering. Both the one who makes men holy and those who are made holy are of the same family. So Jesus is not ashamed to call them brothers. He says,

"I will declare your name to my brothers; in the presence of the congregation I will sing your praises." And again, "I will put my trust in him." And again he says, "Here am I, and the children God has given me."

Since the children have flesh and blood, he too shared in their humanity so that by his death he might destroy him who holds the power of death—that is, the devil—and free those who all their lives were held in slavery by their fear of death. For surely it is not angels he helps, but Abraham's descendants. For this reason he had to be made like his brothers in every way, in order that he might become a merciful and faithful high priest in service to God, and that he might make atonement for the sins of the people.

Angels existed before God created humans; so it stands to reason that God wasn't trying to make *more* angels when he created us. He originally intended for human beings to exist in the Garden of Eden, as Adam and Eve did before the fall. Sin put us out of the garden and out of the kind of fellowship Adam and Eve originally enjoyed with God.

The Bible *never* tells us that we will become angels. Some might point to Matthew 22:30 as evidence that we will be angels in the next life; but read this passage closely: *"At the resurrection people will neither marry nor be given in marriage; they will be like the angels in heaven."*

How will we be like the angels in heaven? In that we will not "marry or be given in marriage." The comparison is limited to the ability to "marry or be given in marriage."

When we die God uses our present bodies as seeds and makes us better humans—not nonhumans.

Are We Trapped Spirits?

Another idea we often hear is that the "real us" is currently trapped by our physical bodies, and that we are spirits waiting to escape our physicality. Gilbert Ryle, author of *The Concept of the Mind*, calls this the "ghost-in-a-machine" theory. Some songs that are popular with Christians today often talk of tearing away our bodies to reveal the "real us."

There were Gnostics in the time of the early church who believed that a great separation existed between the physical and the spiritual. They believed that anything physical was evil, while anything spiritual was good. What's more, the Gnostics believed that the physical was incapable of doing good while the spiritual was incapable of doing bad.

That led the Gnostics to several erroneous conclusions. One was that God could not have created humans or the earth and universe because he was absolutely separate from anything that was physical. Another was a belief that Jesus didn't come to earth in the flesh, but was a spirit or ghost. Because they considered the physical evil, they didn't believe that a perfect God could live in a physical body or be born of a physical woman.

Some Gnostics held the belief that our physical bodies and our spirits were not connected at all and, because of that, people were free to let their bodies follow any physical passion they wished without that action being considered a sin. They believed that the spirit was not responsible for what the body did.

Can a spiritual being sin? Satan's sin got him and the angels that followed him expelled from heaven. They weren't in bodies of flesh, but they sinned nevertheless.

The teachings of Gnosticism have some similarity to the teachings of Buddhism and Hinduism in that the focus is on escaping the physical body to find the imprisoned inner self that exists without the body.

However, the triune nature of humans makes all dimensions of us into one whole. We are spirit, but we are also mind. We are mind, but we are also body. My spirit isn't trapped in a body; it is one with my body and mind.

Adam and Eve were not born with a sinful nature. They contracted it and became out of balance with their original selves. We have inherited that nature from them. You don't have to open your Bible, just turn on the national or international news. Humankind isn't sick and dying only in physical ways. Humanity is sick and dying in mind and spirit as well. Every dimension was affected by the fall that occurred when Adam and Eve sinned.

In the next life we will reunite, not only with God, but also *with ourselves*. Body, mind, and spirit healed and whole.

Will Babies and Small Children Be in Heaven?

I once officiated at a funeral for a child only nine days old. I can't remember the oldest person I've officiated for, but I will never forget the service for that child. Of course, the parents dealt with extremely difficult emotions, including worrying that they had done something incorrectly, that they had somehow killed their child. The autopsy found that the child had a heart defect that no one could have helped, not even the greatest surgeon. That gave them some peace. The greatest peace, however, came with the knowledge that their child would be with Jesus. "Let the little children come to me, and do not forbid them; for of such is the kingdom of heaven" (Matthew 19:14 NKJV).

Jesus never indicated that children would be damned or cast into limbo because they had not yet been baptized, made a public confession, or participated in some other response to God's gift of salvation. He didn't ask those who had no ability to profess faith to confess faith to be saved. In fact, he used children as the example for all of us. "Unless you change and become like little children, you will never enter the kingdom of heaven" (Matthew 18:3). By comparing believers to small children, Jesus showed that God has a tender heart toward little ones who must be dependent on others With no works of their own in which to boast, and no strength to be self-reliant, they'll have nothing but God's mercy when they stand before him. Hmmm. That sounds suspiciously like what it will be like for all of us, no matter how many years we have lived! As stated earlier in this book, Jesus saves those he knows, even if they haven't the ability or opportunity to know him.

Let's look at it another way.

Moses told the Israelites about those who would not be allowed into the Promised Land and those who would be allowed in.

When the LORD heard what you said, he was angry and solemnly swore: "Not a man of this evil generation shall see the good land I swore to give your forefathers, except Caleb son of Jephunneh. He will see it, and I will give him and his descendants the land he set his feet on, because he followed the LORD wholeheartedly."

Because of you the LORD became angry with me also and said, "You shall not enter it, either. But your assistant, Joshua son of Nun, will enter it. Encourage him, because he will lead Israel to inherit it. And the little ones that you said would be taken captive, your children who do not yet know good from bad—they will enter the land. I will give it to them and they will take possession of it. But as for you, turn around and set out toward the desert along the route to the Red Sea."
(Deuteronomy 1:34-40)

Did you see it in verse 39? Moses said God *would* allow innocent children who didn't know right from wrong to enter the Promised Land. It appears that God provides grace to those who "have no knowledge of good and evil."

The punishment of hell is reserved for people who have willingly and knowingly sinned against God (Romans 1:29-31; Galatians 5:19-21; Revelation 21:8). Hell is not for children. Neither is Limbo, a place that some have created in their unique theology to be neither heaven nor hell. Though we live in a sinful, fallen world that is punished because of Adam's sin, salvation is determined individually. Babies and children who pass from this life will go safely to the mighty arms of God.

Some believe that babies who die will be babies or small children for eternity. I don't. In my view, there is no infancy, childhood, or adolescence in heaven. When they get their resurrection bodies, they will be as the resurrection bodies of us all. There won't be infant resurrection bodies or old and frail resurrection bodies. The primary difference would be that those who died extremely young—such as the nine-day-old child mentioned earlier—have no autobiographical memory from their tenure on earth. However, I expect that when they meet their loved ones in heaven, they will learn of their heritage.

Babies and small children are not held responsible for their actions by God because they are without the mental and emotional capacities to knowingly rebel against him. God receives them into heaven and will take very good care of them until they are reunited with their families.

CHAPTER 5
What Happens When Humans Die?

— Dead aware of whats going on on earth.
— Could speak

To protect me from my terror of death, my parents would sometimes avoid driving by graveyards. I was having trouble dealing with the fact that one day my body would stop working and I would die.

I vividly remember a summer day from my young childhood. The Alabama sun blazed as my mother and grandmother walked with me. When my grandmother sat on a bench and watched me play, I took note of her in comparison to my mother. The sun seemed to affect her much more than my mother, and the lines on her face became much more noticeable as her makeup ran in the humidity.

It made me think of death.

Panicked, I told them my fears had returned. My grandmother took me in her arms and she and my mother tried to encourage me by telling me about how wonderful heaven would be. At that young age, I could not imagine anything being better than my current life, and I was scared and angry at the thought of God taking away anyone I loved.

Talking about heaven did not alleviate my emotional state, so my grandmother began tossing me in the air a few inches and catching me. She jokingly said that my fears would be gone when I fell back into her arms.

My fears didn't go anywhere.

As life went on, I learned to adjust to the fear of death in some ways, but I mostly just ignored the issue altogether, going out of my way to pretend it didn't exist.

Several years after that incident, I behaved terribly at my other grandmother's funeral by joking and playing games in an attempt to shield myself from thinking of death and the reality of what had happened. I simply refused to acknowledge it. I understand now why I acted the way I did. I imagine that many children and adults struggle with the reality of death. Perhaps that struggle will not be completely gone until we join God in heaven, but I'm convinced that much of the fear and dread of death can be overcome through the power of God's Word and the Holy Spirit. And by learning about the true heaven.

What Happens After We Die?

Todd looked away from me as he spoke, checking my eyes every now and then to measure my level of skepticism.

"My family took my father's death very hard. Especially my mother," he began. "We have always been very logical people, so that makes this story even more difficult to tell."

Todd's father had been a deacon in his church for many years and only resigned after cancer had ravaged his body to the point that church work became impossible. After he died, his family mourned together and attempted to transition into life without him. Todd went back to Alabama, his brother to Ohio, and his mother to Tennessee.

Todd's mother called him a week after the funeral and told him a fantastic story. According to her, Todd's father had appeared to her just before she fell asleep and gave her a simple "thumbs up" sign before vanishing.

"I think he wants me to know that he's okay," she said to Todd.

Todd humored his mother and told her how glad he was that she could now be at peace with her husband's death.

He dropped the phone on the cradle and shook his head. "Dad's death has really been difficult for her. Now she's seeing things," he thought.

About half an hour later, the phone rang again. This time Todd's brother, Brian, greeted him from the other end.

"I need to tell you something," Brian's voice trembled.

"I saw Dad. I know it sounds crazy, but he gave me a thumbs up and then he was gone."

"Have you talked to mom?" Todd asked.

"Not since the day before yesterday," Brian answered.

Todd didn't know what to think. He knew his family members were not liars and, though people can be fooled by their imaginations, it seemed unlikely that two people on opposite sides of the country could imagine they saw the exact same thing within half an hour of each other.

Odds are you have heard stories similar to Todd's. You may even have one of your own. I used to rationalize away stories like this, conveniently brushing aside such claims as hallucinations or even outright lies. I don't recall having ever said that to a self-proclaimed eyewitness, but I used one of those answers as a silver bullet to assure myself that I had been correctly taught concerning the world of the dead—that they were oblivious and gone for good. I pictured them in some sort of idle, unconscious, comatose state in which they saw nothing but blackness and experienced nothing.

I've come to the point where I don't believe the dead are unaware and out cold. I now believe that events like the one described above, though rare, are possible.

Can you think of a time when a righteous dead person mentioned in the Bible *didn't* know what was happening on earth? A quick tour of biblical references to the righteous dead demonstrates their alertness and awareness. They knew the events happening on earth, sometimes even bringing messages about the future.

Let's glimpse three examples.

The first comes from the Old Testament era. When King Saul urged the witch of Endor to bring Samuel from the dead, he thought

94

Samuel could help him. But when Samuel arrived, things didn't go quite as Saul planned.

> Samuel said to Saul, "Why have you disturbed me by bringing me up?" "I am in great distress," Saul said. "The Philistines are fighting against me, and God has turned away from me. He no longer answers me, either by prophets or by dreams. So I have called on you to tell me what to do."
>
> Samuel said, "Why do you consult me, now that the LORD has turned away from you and become your enemy? The LORD has done what he predicted through me. The LORD has torn the kingdom out of your hands and given it to one of your neighbors—to David. Because you did not obey the LORD or carry out his fierce wrath against the Amalekites, the LORD has done this to you today. The LORD will hand over both Israel and you to the Philistines, and tomorrow you and your sons will be with me. The LORD will also hand over the army of Israel to the Philistines." (1 Samuel 28:15-19)

Samuel knew Saul was fighting the Philistines. When Saul stated his purpose for wanting to talk with him, Samuel's reply showed thorough knowledge of the situation. He used words like "now" and "the Lord has torn the kingdom out of your hands and given it to David." He knew everything that was happening and things that were about to happen. He even told Saul that he would die the next day in battle with the Philistines.

Samuel lived in the world of the dead, not inhabiting this earth, but he knew what was happening on earth among the living.

The next example comes from the New Testament. When Jesus attempted to discuss his impending death with Peter, James, and John, they gave him no support. Peter urged him not to go through with it, angering Jesus with his words (Matthew 16:21-23). Shortly after that, two leaders from the past, Moses and Elijah, came to Jesus and spoke with him about his death. "As he was praying, the appearance of his face changed, and his clothes became as bright as a flash of lightning. Two men, Moses and Elijah, appeared in glorious splendor, talking with Jesus. They spoke about his departure, which he was about to bring to fulfillment at Jerusalem" (Luke 9:29-31).

Notice that Luke says "two men" appeared to Jesus. Not two ghosts. Not two angels. Not two spirits. Two men. Note also that Luke says they appeared in "glorious splendor." This is consistent with our new bodies being described as "glorious" in 1 Corinthians 15. Both Moses and Elijah knew what was happening on earth; each knew that Jesus was about to bring the law and prophets to fulfillment in Jerusalem. Moses and Elijah lived with God in heaven yet they knew of the events occurring on earth.

The third example comes from heaven itself. It doesn't tell of a righteous dead person returning to earth to speak with a living person. Instead, it tells of the righteous dead praying while in heaven. Here is what John saw:

"When he opened the fifth seal, I saw under the altar the souls of those who had been slain because of the word of God and the testimony they had maintained. They called out in a loud voice, 'How long, Sovereign Lord, holy and true, until you judge the inhabitants of the earth and avenge our blood?' Then each of them was given a white robe, and they were told to wait a little longer, until the number of their fellow servants and brothers who were to be killed as they had been was completed." (Revelation 6:9-11)

The martyrs knew they had not been avenged on earth. They were told to wait until the right time and that vengeance would surely come.

The martyrs lived with Moses, Elijah, Samuel, and others in the presence of God. They weren't here on earth, but they knew what was happening on earth. Their blood had not been avenged and they prayed for God to avenge it.

It appears that the righteous dead have knowledge of the happenings on earth. Can they see the earth, or do they just know because the information is made known in heaven? I don't know. Along with many Christians, I believe that Hebrews 12:1 teaches that the righteous dead have personal access to what occurs here. After saying that the "world was not worthy" of heroes of faith such as David, Samuel, Gideon, and others in the previous chapter, the writer of Hebrews says, "Therefore, since we are surrounded by such a great cloud of witnesses, let us throw off everything that hinders and the sin that so easily entangles, and let us run with perseverance the race marked out for us" (12:1). David, Samuel, Gideon, and others are listed as part of a cloud of witnesses around us.

It's comforting to know that "a great cloud of witnesses" watches us and knows many of the things we do. Even if they can't see it occurring, they at least have knowledge of earthly events. It's comforting in that I feel that I can connect in some small ways with loved ones who have died. I'm not saying that I can have live conversations with them, but I can still show them honor in this life and know that it's very possible they will be aware of my continued respect and love for them.

In addition to being comforting, I admit that I also feel some positive peer pressure from this cloud of witnesses. I want my grandparents to be proud of me. I want my father to know that the things he taught me have influenced me and continue to help me be a better person. I want Paul to see me following the teachings that the Holy Spirit inspired him to write down. So in many ways, I feel accountable to that cloud of witnesses and that helps me serve God better.

The Bible also tells us that the righteous dead still pray and do so effectively. When the saints in Revelation 6 prayed that God would avenge them on the earth, they made a specific request and were consoled to wait for the answer they desired. I would think that they pray for more than vengeance on those who killed them. Because they know what's happening on earth and continue to pray, I have no trouble believing that they pray for us. If anyone in heaven is praying for me, I imagine they receive just as quick and direct an answer as those praying in Revelation 6.

These passages led me to believe that my grandmother knows what happens here. She is part of that "cloud of witnesses" surrounding me as I run my race. I haven't any doubt that in heaven she prays for me as well as the other members of her family. How much more powerful the prayers of the righteous dead must be without the filters of human doubt!

Have I made it clear? I strongly believe that the dead know what is happening here. I believe that strongly enough that I'll ask you a favor. If for some reason I were to die soon, I want you to take a message to my children for me. At my funeral, console my children and grandchildren with this chapter. Read my words to them.

Tell them I love them and that I'll watch them throughout their lives. I'll hurt when they struggle. I'll rejoice in their triumphs. I'll cry at their weddings. Tell them that when they feel extra strength come from God, their daddy or granddaddy is praying for them. Just because he now lives in heaven doesn't mean he has forgotten them.

Tell them I'll hurt with them as they learn the tough side of life. I'll swell with pride at their successes. I'll gaze lovingly at all of my grandchildren and great-grandchildren if this world lasts that long.

When you tell my mentally handicapped daughter, Angela, she'll have the toughest time understanding what you mean and the easiest time believing it, once she sorts it out in her way. Her simplicity seems to keep her closer to heaven than the rest of us.

If the Dead Are Aware of Our Struggles, How Is It Heaven?

I remember sitting at the funeral of my Aunt Darlene. Though the tremendous pain of cancer had invaded the last few years of her life, she always seemed to have a smile on her face and an unusually pleasant attitude. She was indeed the "salt of the earth." I miss her very much.

As I sat at her funeral, a song that her family requested played for the solemn crowd. You may have heard the song. It's called, "There Are Holes in the Floors of Heaven," sung by Steve Wariner and other artists. As you might expect from the title, the song tells the story of loved ones in heaven watching over us. The story is of a young child asking about his mother in heaven.

While listening to that song at Darlene's funeral, it seemed stingingly depressing yet strangely hopeful. She had left behind two sons. One was very young, and I ached when I thought of how he had only had a few years with his mother and would face the rest of his childhood without her. Yet the song reinforced the comfort that she would be watching over him. She wouldn't miss his first love, his graduation, or the birth of his children. She will be a witness to all those events if she chooses (and I'm sure she will).

A question usually surfaces from the discussion of loved ones being aware even after death. Often I'll hear, "But how can the Bible say there won't be crying or pain in heaven? Surely, if our loved ones are aware of the bad things that happen to us, it wouldn't really be heaven."

I certainly understand the reasoning behind the question, but I think it is asked without certain points being considered. After all, God is well aware of what is happening on earth, yet it is still heaven for him. The angels are also aware of what is happening on earth, yet it is still heaven for them. When Jesus lived on earth, he mourned and grieved for the people on earth (Matthew 23:37-39; John 11:33-36), but that does not mean that in heaven Jesus is now incapable of mourning for us or sympathizing with us when we encounter life's troubles.

The Bible does not say there won't be crying or mourning in heaven. Instead, it tells us that God "will wipe every tear" from our eyes when "the old order of things has passed away."

Then I saw a new heaven and a new earth, for the first heaven and the first earth had passed away, and there was no longer any sea. I saw the Holy City, the new Jerusalem, coming down out of heaven from God, prepared as a bride beautifully dressed for her husband. And I heard a loud voice from the throne saying, "Now the dwelling of God is with men, and he will live with them. They will be his people, and God himself will be with them and be their God. He will wipe every tear from their eyes. There will be no more death or mourning or crying or pain, for the old order of things has passed away." (Revelation 21:1-4)

Our loved ones are in waiting for the fulfillment of the resurrection of the dead, as well as the end of this earth. Until "the old order of things has passed away," there are still reasons to mourn. But I suspect they will be blessed with a much clearer perspective of the bigger picture. God is there to comfort them, and they understand that certain things must happen before we can be with them.

In the sense used in the song, I think that there are "holes in the floor of heaven." Parents can know about their children, children can know about their parents, a spouse can know about the one left behind, and friends can know about friends. What happens on earth is still very important to them because we are here.

Where Will the Dead Be Before the Resurrection?

The natural order of things would seem to place this section before the discussion of our resurrection bodies. However, it seemed to me that we couldn't discuss this subject without first establishing the concept of the resurrection body and that that body will have form and substance.

As you're likely aware, there are different views concerning the dead prior to the resurrection. One view is that the souls of the dead hibernate or sleep while waiting for the resurrection. I guess that would be somewhat like saving a computer file onto a CD. The file would be saved until needed again, and then it would be retrieved. In this case, a soul would be stored in the mind of God and then revived on the day of resurrection. A friend of mine writes extensively on this view. I respect him deeply, but I find this view difficult to accept because of the many examples in the Bible of the dead being conscious, active, and aware (1 Samuel 28:15-19; Luke 9:29-31; 16:22-31; Revelation 6:9-11).

Also, in Matthew 22:31-32 Jesus said to the Sadducees: "But about the resurrection of the dead—have you not read what God said to you, 'I am the God of Abraham, the God of Isaac, and the God of Jacob'? He is not the God of the dead but of the living." Jesus listed Abraham, Isaac, and Jacob among the living. He didn't say they were unaware or filed away somewhere. He called them "the living."

It is correct that in some passages, such as 1 Thessalonians 4:13-17, the Bible refers to the dead as having "fallen asleep." Jesus himself used that terminology when telling the apostles that Lazarus had died. I see that as no different from our current euphemisms for death. In the Deep South, for example, we say that someone "passed" or has "gone on." It is not unusual for a culture to choose other, less harsh words for death. However, as already pointed out repeatedly, the examples we have of the dead show that they are conscious and active. I think it is consistent to say that "asleep" refers to the outward appearance of the body in death. It appears to be asleep in that the eyes are closed and the body is completely still. The earthly physical part of us "sleeps" until it is used as seed for our new bodies and reunited with our spirit at the resurrection. We continue to live on without the body, meaning that we are in a very real sense incomplete until we receive the resurrection body when Jesus returns. (In my book *Seeing the Unseen* I give a more detailed Bible study about why the dead crave bodies.)

The Value of This Life

It's common for some to speak disparagingly about this life in an attempt to sound spiritual and enlightened. They act as though this life is simply an ongoing torture that forces their eyes to open each morning. This viewpoint, like the Gnostic idea that our body is simply a dungeon trapping our spirits, may sound poetic, righteous, and deep, but that does not make it so.

If we look at the life of Jesus, we see a very different picture. He healed people physically as well as spiritually. If this life really didn't matter, why did he bother healing people physically? Why didn't he just say, "All that matters is the next life! I don't want to waste my time on the physical"?

Furthermore, Jesus brought two people back from death. Lazarus walked out of the tomb after four days (John 11:43-44), and Jesus caused the dead daughter of "the ruler" to open her eyes and sit up (Mark 9:23-25). If this life did not have importance, why did Jesus bother to bring them back from the "afterlife" to the worthlessness of this life?

This is not to say that this life is as important as the eternal life we will experience afterwards. Colossians 3:2 says, "Set your mind on the things above. . . ." Yet at the same time, the Bible says in Genesis that God delighted in the creation of human beings out of the soil, and that when God looked at all of his creation he pronounced it very good (Genesis 1-2). The New Testament views our bodies as temples of the

Spirit and sacred offerings to God (1 Corinthians 3:16-17, Romans 12:1). God chose to become a human being with a real body (1 Timothy 3:16). The human body is so important to God that he plans to transform it and preserve it eternally (1 Corinthians 15:42-49).

God expects us to take this life seriously and to assign it the level of importance it is due as a gift and calling from him.

We must fulfill our responsibilities on earth, while at the same time fulfilling our responsibilities to the next life. Paul says, "Whatever you do, work at it with all your heart, as working for the Lord, not for men, since you know that you will receive an inheritance from the Lord as a reward. It is the Lord Christ you are serving" (Colossians 3:23-24).

We should consider life a service to God. We are to live with a higher standard than the rest of the world. While the rest of the world works for bosses, we are to work at our jobs as if for God and do our very best for him, no matter what we do. If we are lazy when it's time to work, we aren't only short-changing our employer, we short-change God. He gave us life and expects us to use the talents and abilities he gave us as best we can.

This life provides memories for eternity. Don't take it for granted, but at the same time, remember that God has even more awaiting us.

CHAPTER 6
Where Is Heaven?

Okay, I'll admit it. I've always been a Trekkie. From a young age I wanted to go boldly where no man had gone before, just as the crew aboard the Star Trek Enterprise did on my television. Captain Kirk lived out some of my dreams as he landed on distant planets and flew past the countless stars in our massive universe. When I was in kindergarten, my parents, friends, and teachers knew I wanted to be an astronaut when I grew up. My parents took me to the U.S. Space and Rocket Center in Huntsville, Alabama, more times than I can remember, and I actually liked the freeze-dried "Astronaut Ice Cream" that we bought on each visit.

Most people seem to have at least some curiosity about the universe. Today we call it outer space. In Paul's day, they called it the "second heaven." In their view, the first heaven was the atmosphere around the earth, the second heaven held the stars, and the third heaven served as the location of God's dwelling.

When the biblical text says "heaven," it might mean any of those three areas depending on the context of the particular passage. We need to know which "heaven" the Bible describes as we read.

Usually when the Bible uses the plural of heaven, it is referring either to the atmosphere or outer space. When it is singular, it usually refers to the location of God's dwelling. But that's not always the case, especially when considering the differences between versions of the Bible.

Some Examples of the Word Heaven

Some of the newer versions of the Bible translate "heaven" as air, whereas the older versions and the New King James Version typically use the singular of the word "heaven."

For example, Job 35:10-11 reads: "But no one says, 'Where is God my Maker, who gives songs in the night, who teaches more to us than to the beasts of the earth and makes us wiser than the birds of the air?'" Air is the word of choice for the New International Version and the New Revised Standard, while the King James and New King James say "heaven."

The second use of "heaven," what we call outer space today, is translated in Genesis 1:14 as "expanse of the sky" by the New International Version, as "dome of the sky" by the New Revised Standard, as "firmament of the heaven" by the King James Version, and as "firmament of the heavens" by the New King James Version.

The third heaven, God's dwelling, is most often translated as "heaven." An example is 2 Chronicles 7:14, which reads: "If my people, who are called by my name, will humble themselves and pray and seek my face and turn from their wicked ways, then will I hear from heaven and forgive their sin and will heal their land."

Heaven's Location

Who knows where heaven is? The Bible simply does not tell us, and the universe is much too vast for us to pinpoint an exact or approximate location.

I can assume, however, that heaven is somewhere in the universe because when Jesus left for heaven, he ascended. When we travel "up," on earth we are really going "out." Jesus went into outer space on his way to heaven. That's about all we can presume concerning the present location of heaven, but as you'll see in the next section, heaven will one day relocate.

It seems clear from the Bible that the future location of heaven will be on the New Earth.

A New Earth?

When discussing the topic of heaven and the next life with Christians, I've noticed that there are two topics that seem to get people thinking: the glorified human body and the New Earth. When those two concepts click in someone's head, their entire perspective on heaven and the next life often changes.

I recall a conversation about heaven with my uncle who is an avid golfer. He had seen some of my writings and told me that after reading them, he was looking forward to heaven. He, too, had held the eternal-church-service-of-the-bodiless view. As we talked, he said that a few days after he had finished reading my earlier writings he began to realize the implications.

"It occurred to me that I will actually play golf again!" he said with excitement.

Because I also dearly love the game of golf, I felt emotion stir within me as he spoke. Golf means a lot to my family. My dad, uncle, cousin, brother, and a certain in-law have had many great memories playing golf together. Some of the deepest conversations and closest bonding I've ever experienced with them has happened while on the golf course. Also, as any golfer will tell you, there are certain shots and putts that make me smile or even break into laughter when I remember them. The golfing experience to us is more than a game.

I grinned from ear to ear as we talked about being able to play again on the New Earth. To him it meant that he would be able to swing a golf club with the power of the youthful body that had earned him a college scholarship. It meant that he could play without the pain of tendonitis or "golfer's elbow." That made him happy. I felt joy thinking that my dad could play again with his grandfather who introduced him to the game.

If that sounds shallow to you or doesn't fit your picture of heaven, then I haven't done a very good job so far in this book. When God created humans, he created the ideal place for them. If humans hadn't violated God's law, we would still be living in a worldwide Garden of Eden. After all, Eden was where God originally placed Adam; but

Adam and Eve were told to "be fruitful and increase in number; fill the earth and subdue it." So their stomping ground wasn't limited just to the Garden of Eden. There may have been many other gardens around the earth. God meant the entire earth to be ours, good for growing food and for all the joys of living.

When Adam and Eve ate of the fruit of the Tree of Knowledge of Good and Evil, they fundamentally changed the paradise in which they lived.

Corrupted Humanity, Corrupted Earth

Sin brought many changes. Before the fall, for example, being naked was connected to sin. It was how God created the first humans and he required no covering of them. Yet after eating of the fruit, Adam hid from God. When God called to him, Adam answered, "'I heard you in the garden, and I was afraid because I was naked; so I hid.' And he [God] said, 'Who told you that you were naked? Have you eaten from the tree that I commanded you not to eat from?'" (Genesis 3:11).

Adam and Eve felt they had to cover their sinfulness, whereas previously they were naked and unashamed. Before eating the fruit, they saw no difference between an uncovered hand, whose purposes included grasping food, and the parts of the body designed for them to "be fruitful and multiply." While sinless, no body part was shameful, nor did anything need to be covered.

Then they gained the knowledge of "good and evil." Why did that make them feel their nakedness was something to hide?

Some believe it was because they realized what lust was, and felt the need to cover up to prevent that. However, Adam and Eve were given to each other by God and feeling sexual desire for each other was not sinful or embarrassing. *He* made them male and female. I think it highly probable that they'd already been having sexual relations with each other before the fall because God told them to "be fruitful and increase in number" (Genesis 1:22). Do we really think that they ignored (thereby, disobeying) that command during their time together before the fall? Look at the context:

> Then God said, "Let us make man in our image, in our likeness, and let them rule over the fish of the sea and the birds of the air, over the livestock, over all the earth, and over all the creatures that move along the ground."
>
> So God created man in his own image, in the image of God he created him; male and female he created them.
>
> God blessed them and said to them, "Be fruitful and increase in number; fill the earth and subdue it. Rule over the fish of the sea and the birds of the air and over every living creature that moves on the ground."
>
> Then God said, "I give you every seed-bearing plant on the face of the whole earth and every tree that has fruit with seed in it. They will be yours for food. And to all the beasts of the earth and all the birds of the air and all the creatures that move on

the ground—everything that has the breath of life in it—I give every green plant for food." And it was so. (Genesis 1:26-30)

I don't recall hearing anyone question whether Adam and Eve ruled over all animal and plant life before the fall. The passage above told them to do so and we assume they did. Then why not assume that they also followed the command to "be fruitful and multiply"? God told Eve that, as a consequence of her sin, "I will greatly increase your pain in childbearing; with pain you will give birth to children. Your desire will be for your husband, and he will rule over you" (Genesis 3:16).

It would seem that for this statement to have power, she would have had to already had children. Maybe that's why when her first son was born, she said, "With the help of the Lord I have brought forth a man" (Genesis 4:1). Could it be that she had already brought forth women? The age-old question, "Where did Cain get his wife?" may well be answered by this insight. Female children may already have been born before the fall, so that after the fall Eve's pain in delivery was "greatly increased."

To me it doesn't seem reasonable that Adam and Eve wanted to cover themselves because they suddenly discovered sexual desire.

Others have said that their shame and need to cover themselves came directly from the knowledge of good and evil they gained from the forbidden fruit. That new knowledge forced them to decide what was good and what was evil. They looked at their nakedness and decided there was something wrong with it.

That solution doesn't make sense to me because they knew that God accepted their nudity. There is no sin in being nude with one's mate. And if God seeing us naked is a sin, then we're all doomed because God sees everything! "From heaven the LORD looks down and sees all mankind; from his dwelling place he watches all who live on earth" (Psalms 33:13-14).

The text provides the reason: they were ashamed and wanted to hide. Covering themselves was an act of trying to shield themselves from God seeing and knowing everything about them. From that point, humanity would be plagued by secrets, shame, and hiding—physically, mentally, and spiritually.

The point is that because of sin, Adam and Eve changed. They now feared the previous intimacy they had experienced with their Father. They knew evil now, and that knowledge led them to run *from* God rather than *to* him. Because they were the first humans, their changes affected all humanity that would spring from their loins.

Humans changed. God changed his relationship with them. Life changed to include sickness and death. Man no longer ruled the earth. He fell from supremacy to fear. The earth itself changed. All that was perfect was perfect no more.

God Destroyed the Earth

God destroyed the earth. You read that right. God destroyed the earth and then gave us a new earth. Read it for yourself in Genesis 6:11-13:

Now the earth was corrupt in God's sight and was full of violence. God saw how corrupt the earth had become, for all
the people on earth had corrupted their ways. So God said
to Noah, "I am going to put an end to all people, for the earth
is filled with violence because of them. I am surely going to
destroy both them and the earth. So make yourself an ark of
cypress wood."

God sent a flood to destroy "both them and the earth." However, God
didn't destroy "all people" or "the earth" in the way we might define the
word "destroy." God spared not just one man, but an entire family. He
didn't destroy the earth in the sense that it would never exist again.
God purged and purified the earth of those who were not his.

The Apostle Peter reminds us of God's destruction using the flood
waters and tells us that God will use fire to destroy the earth to make
the New Earth that will exist in harmony with the New Heaven.

First of all, you must understand that in the last days scoffers
will come, scoffing and following their own evil desires. They
will say, "Where is this 'coming' he promised? Ever since our
fathers died, everything goes on as it has since the beginning
of creation." But they deliberately forget that long ago by God's
word the heavens existed and the earth was formed out of
water and by water. By these waters also the world of that time
was deluged and destroyed. By the same word the present

heavens and earth are reserved for fire, being kept for the day of judgment and destruction of ungodly men. (2 Peter 3:3-7)

It's quite possible that the coming destruction of the earth will be like the flood in that God will purify the earth of "ungodly men," changing the earth without obliterating the earth. Peter writes that the flood destroyed the earth, yet we know that the earth itself was not done away with by the flood. In a real sense it was destroyed, but not in the sense of annihilation. If God wishes to completely destroy it and make an entirely new earth, that's fine with me. However, many believe that, rather than the earth being annihilated, it will be purified by fire just as it was once purified by water, as the passage above suggests. Destroying the earth by fire will be similar to the way God destroyed the earth by flood.

What about the language about the stars, moon, and those types of things being done away with? God used similar language in reference to Babylon's destruction (Isaiah 13) and of Edom's destruction (Isaiah 34). Look at the word about Edom (the country established by Jacob's brother Esau): "All the stars of the heavens will be dissolved and the sky rolled up like a scroll; all the starry host will fall like withered leaves from the vine, like shriveled figs from the fig tree" (Isaiah 34:4). God destroyed Edom but the stars didn't dissolve or the sky roll up in a literal way. The destruction was so complete that for Edom it was as if the universe was dissolved. I think it likely that the words of 2 Peter may be used similarly when it speaks of the present earth being "reserved for fire." God will purify the earth of sin before he sets up his throne on earth. Paul says in 1 Corinthians 7:31 that "this world in its present form is passing away."

The things that glorify and please God will be given new form. It won't be just our resurrection bodies that will be new and incorruptible; the earth will be made new and incorruptible as well. Consider Romans 8:19: "The creation waits in eager expectation for the sons of God to be revealed." Creation, not just humanity, waits eagerly to be restored to the original beauty and splendor that God intended. "For the creation was subjected to frustration, not by its own choice, but by the will of the one who subjected it, in hope that the creation itself will be liberated from its bondage to decay and brought into the glorious freedom of the children of God" (Romans 8:20-21).

Liberation and annihilation usually don't get listed together. To liberate is to set free. Creation anticipates its freedom from bondage and decay. According to this passage, creation shares a similar future with the children of God. "We know that the whole creation has been groaning as in the pains of childbirth right up to the present time. Not only so, but we ourselves, who have the firstfruits of the Spirit, groan inwardly as we wait eagerly for our adoption as sons, the redemption of our bodies" (Romans 8:22-23). Along with "the whole creation," we wait for "redemption." We wait for "the redemption of our bodies." Creation waits for the redemption of its original design.

It appears that on this same earth, we will reign with Christ. The earth will be renewed, purified, and resurrected, just as will God's people.

Perhaps the earth groans through its earthquakes, hurricanes, and tornados. The continents literally move beneath our feet and volcanoes erupt with furious heat. Not just the earth, but as things are now the whole creation moves inexorably toward destruction. Black holes vacuum the unimaginable. Stars collide. Entire galaxies crash into each other causing unthinkably massive explosions beyond our ability to grasp. Creation is indeed groaning!

The Restoration

We're told that just as God raised Jesus from the dead and gave him a new and glorious body making him the second Adam (1 Corinthians 15:20-23), God will also raise our bodies, our earth, and our universe to the magnificent ideals of his original intent.

This next passage is extremely important to our study: "He must remain in heaven until the time comes for God to restore everything, as he promised long ago through his holy prophets" (Acts 3:21). God will restore everything. We will live on a New Earth that is the restoration of the first earth—the one before Adam and Eve sinned.

Once the earth is purified by fire, God will bring heaven and earth together. He will reign on his throne forever with his people and his creation. And God will grant us access to the Tree of Life once again. And everything will be good, as it was in the beginning.

> Then I saw a new heaven and a new earth, for the first heaven and the first earth had passed away, and there was no longer any sea. I saw the Holy City, the new Jerusalem, coming down

out of heaven from God, prepared as a bride beautifully dressed for her husband. And I heard a loud voice from the throne saying, "Now the dwelling of God is with men, and he will live with them. They will be his people, and God himself will be with them and be their God. He will wipe every tear from their eyes. There will be no more death or mourning or crying or pain, for the old order of things has passed away."

He who was seated on the throne said, "I am making everything new!" Then he said, "Write this down, for these words are trustworthy and true."

He said to me: "It is done. I am the Alpha and the Omega, the Beginning and the End. To him who is thirsty I will give to drink without cost from the spring of the water of life." (Revelation 21:1-6)

CHAPTER 7
Life on the New Earth

The way that I used to view heaven made it a depressing topic. Why should we discuss it? Why dwell on what happens in the so-called afterlife? Isn't heaven just the parting gift for dying? Isn't it simply to give us a little more peace when death's bed finally comes?

I must admit that, for a time, I refused to think about heaven except when contemplating a deceased loved one. I didn't want to imagine that person lying in a grave and I didn't want to think I'd never see him or her again. During those mental meanderings, heaven served as a great distraction. I could simply stick my dead loved ones in a vague, dream-like heaven in my mind and take them out whenever I chose to entertain the idea that they weren't *completely* dead. I made heaven blurry and mysterious enough that I didn't have to deal with what may or may not be true. That way I could hold off death and the thought of death as long as possible.

Why?

I've been afraid of death. Maybe you have as well.

What about death terrifies us so much? Is that fear simply a natural instinct placed within us to keep us alive as long as possible? Is it because we don't *really* believe in a next life? Is it because we aren't confident of our standing with God? Is it that we're afraid of losing all that we've worked for and having to start over? Or is it mainly the fear of the unknown?

Many have struggled with at least one of those fears when thinking about heaven.

It is perfectly natural to try to avoid death, even if we believe heaven waits on the other side. We were created to despise and run from death. If we weren't, I can't imagine how the human species would still exist. Some of us have been in life or death situations, and the "fight or flight" adrenaline rush gave us the extra focus and strength needed to protect our own lives or the life of another.

I'll be very open with you. I want to live for years and years to come. I want to experience special moments with my family and friends. That's okay. If God didn't want us to enjoy life, he wouldn't have created us to do so. If God didn't want us in this life anymore, he could return right now and put an end to it all. But God's timing is not my timing. I have no right to interrupt or help him along with the process of taking me to heaven.

This Life Is a Learning Opportunity

This life is important. It matters and should be appreciated and valued. Why? Perhaps an illustration will help me explain.

As a teenager, I wanted little more than to drive a car. I watched as my friends turned driving age and could barely contain my eagerness to grasp the steering wheel of a powerful, modern-day machine. You can imagine my frustration when my time came to drive and my dad chose a church parking lot for my training. I flippantly made the turns, stops, and maneuvers he required until he offered some wisdom for my consideration.

"Son," he began, "if you can't prove to me that you can handle this vehicle at slow speeds in a small parking lot, what would make me think you can safely navigate it at high speeds with other cars only a few feet away? Furthermore, if you won't take training seriously, how can I know that you'll ever take driving seriously?"

We see this principle throughout life. It's usually the minor leagues before the majors. It's basic training before active wartime assignments. And it's this life before eternity with God.

On this earth we learn many lessons that will be valuable in heaven. We learn how to work, study, and, most importantly, how to love God in spite of the fact that God doesn't always do what we wish. All those lessons will be useful in heaven.

Will We Know Everything in Heaven?

There seems to be a popular perception that we will know everything there is to know when we get to heaven. This belief persists despite the fact that it is widely accepted that humans die without perfect knowledge and that God alone is perfect in knowledge. The assumption is that all this knowledge and understanding will be given to us at the resurrection of the dead and the return of Jesus Christ. Typically, this passage is cited:

> For we know in part and we prophesy in part, but when perfection comes, the imperfect disappears. When I was a child, I talked like a child, I thought like a child, I reasoned like a child. When I became a man, I put childish ways behind me. Now we see but a poor reflection as in a mirror; then we shall see face to face. Now I know in part; then I shall know fully, even as I am fully known. (1 Corinthians 13:9-12)

Did Paul mean for us to infer from those words that we will know everything? Or did he mean that our understanding of God will no longer be distorted in our perceptions, and that we will finally see God face to face? If it means that we will know everything, it equates us with God himself. Only God knows everything and, therefore, is omniscient. To see clearly and have a greater understanding is one thing, but to be omniscient like God is another. The angels in heaven don't know everything and neither will glorified humans who live in heaven on the New Earth.

We will, however, be constantly learning. Heaven won't be a stagnant world. It will be a fresh, stimulating, and challenging frontier where we will develop an ever-deepening understanding of God's greatness. We will continue to grow, change, learn, and mature without sin to weigh us down and deter us.

I wouldn't want it any other way.

Can you imagine a world in which you knew everything? A world with no mystery, no adventure, and no unfulfilled dream? We were created by God to learn, study, think, experiment, theorize, discuss, and examine. How incredibly boring it would be to have every challenge and question removed from our existence. We could never look forward to knowing something new and fresh.

Only God has the capacity to know absolutely everything there is to know. He possesses that capacity because he is God. Only God lives without anything new or unexpected. Why? Because he is the Creator, and we are the created. He is the painter, and we are the painting. We exist in the world he made, not vice versa. He is the potter, we are the clay. He is the teacher, we are the students.

We weren't created to have all knowledge and understanding, but God has always had it and always will.

Is This World My Home?

Maybe you won't be surprised to learn that I started humming the words to an old Christian song as soon as I typed the words above.

This world is not my home, I'm just a passing through.
My treasures are laid up somewhere beyond the blue.
The angels beckon me from heaven's open door
and I can't feel at home in this world anymore.

I remember singing this song in church as a small child. The words reminded me that this life might be tough, and even terrible at times, but one day God would welcome me into a place that wasn't earth. A place where all my dreams could come true.

That sounded wonderful, but something didn't add up.

Why would God put me on this earth, only to take me to another place entirely when my time here ended? Why two places? Why did God put humans here in the first place if we belonged somewhere else?

As a child I never asked those questions of anyone, but I listened to the answers when others asked similar questions. Sometimes the answers consisted of the semi-Gnostic philosophies. The explanation would often be that we really didn't belong in a body to begin with, and God would rescue our spirits from our bodies when Jesus returned to take those spirits to heaven where they belonged.

However, the very first book of the Bible triggered questions about that: Why did God create a place for us if it was the wrong place for us to begin with? Why did God create a human if humans would one day become extinct and morphed into another being altogether? Bottom line: If God considered his creation to be good upon completion (Genesis 1:31), why would he change his mind later? Why did God create Adam and Eve to live forever on earth as humans, but then decide we would be better off as spirits living in a different realm?

As you know from previous chapters, I don't believe that we will simply be spirits in the next life. If that were the case, then we could say that when God created humans in the beginning to live forever in a body it was a mistake. The fact that God originally intended for us to live on earth forever as humans is very important to this study. In Adam and the garden we see the design as God originally intended. Adam and Eve were not created to die. They were to be stewards of the earth, and God supplied them with the Tree of Life so that they would be able to live forever.

Note the lingering effects of the Tree of Life on humans:

This is the written account of Adam's line. When God created man, he made him in the likeness of God. He created them male and female and blessed them .... Adam lived 930 years, and then he died .... Seth lived 912 years .... Enosh lived 905 years .... Kenan lived 910 years .... Mahalalel lived 895 years .... Jared lived 962 years .... Enoch lived 365 years. Enoch walked with God; then he was no more, because God took him away .... Methuselah lived 969 years .... Lamech lived 777 years, and then he died. (Genesis 5:1-31)

By the time David wrote, the lifespan had dropped dramatically.

The length of our days is seventy years—
    or eighty, if we have the strength;
    yet their span is but trouble and sorrow,
    for they quickly pass, and we fly away. (Psalms 90:10)

Life spans aren't much more than that even now. It seems that when the effects of the Tree of Life finally were no longer inherent in human bodies, we found ourselves in that seventy to eighty year range. Modern medicine and vitamins help, but they are nothing compared to the Tree of Life!

The Tree of Life serves as a strong indication that God planned for humans to live forever on the earth. He didn't make a mistake by putting human beings on this planet.

Without God Humankind Didn't Fare So Well

Satan tempted Adam and Eve with an offer they thought they couldn't refuse—godhood. He didn't offer them the ability to create galaxies or life forms in mere seconds, but something almost as tempting—knowledge.

"You will not surely die," the serpent said to the woman. "For God knows that when you eat of it your eyes will be opened, and you will be like God, knowing good and evil." When the woman saw that the fruit of the tree was good for food and pleasing to the eye, and also desirable for gaining wisdom, she took some and ate it. She also gave some to her husband, who was with her, and he ate it. (Genesis 3:4-6)

Satan convinced Eve that she was missing something the way God created her; he twisted God's words to make her believe that God wanted to hold her back. He deceived her into believing that she could be her own god.

By taking away the Tree of Life and casting humankind from the garden, God in essence gave this message: "Apparently you think you can be like me. I'll take back my garden paradise and turn the control of the earth over to you. You'll be in charge of getting food to grow from the earth. You'll be in charge of keeping peace among all the people that you bring forth. And while you're at it, be god over your health and life. Let me know how that goes."

History cries out that humans cannot sustain themselves without God. We failed miserably at the task of being our own god. That fact becomes painfully clear when we pass by cemeteries and hospitals. We possess knowledge of good and evil. We are able to procreate new life, certainly not equal to creation, but we can make more people. There are traits that we share with God, but they aren't enough.

Our shortcomings are much too great.

We are unable to force the earth to do our will. Sure, we get close by growing food out of the earth, drilling for oil to refine, clearing forests for roads and buildings, and having some control over other life forms on the earth. Nevertheless, the wind and water do not obey our very words as they did when Jesus calmly demanded they stop all the commotion (Luke 8:22-25). And we have to protect ourselves from the heat and cold by seeking some form of shelter.

We also fall terribly short in an area over which we have very little control—our lives. We can't sustain ourselves forever. Only God can provide and maintain eternal life. We can't.

Truly, we make pathetic gods.

God's message from the Bible is, "If you so choose, I'll be your God again as I was in the beginning. I'll provide you with eternal life—again. I'll restore fellowship between you and me. I'll take control of the earth again."

This world was our home until we distorted and stained it, but God offers to make everything new. Just as God washed us clean and made us new, he will renew the earth and restore it to his original intent—to be a perfect home for us, a home where he will live with us as our God.

God raises us from the dead and brings a New Heaven to the New Earth.

What Will the New Earth Be Like?

The restored earth will retain many of the things that make it earth. The New Earth will have trees, rivers, mountains, and vegetation.

Just as human beings may maintain identifying marks in heaven such as certain physical features, the New Earth may have some, if not all, of the natural wonders that it possesses now. It could be that one day you stand with a friend on a mountain on the New Earth and say, "Do you remember when we hiked up this mountain when it was the old earth and saw that beautiful field? Let's go see what it looks like now!"

As C. S. Lewis said, ". . . the hills and valleys of heaven will be to those you now experience not as a copy is to an original, nor as a substitute is to the genuine article, but as the flower to the root, or the diamond to the coal." [C. S. Lewis, *Letters to Malcolm: Chiefly on Prayer* (New York: Harcourt Brace Jovanovich, 1963), 84]

If you want clues to what eternal life will be like, look around. Heaven will be located on the New Earth, and we will be able to live in the earthly paradise God originally intended for us. Just as God redeemed us from sin, he will redeem the earth from its curse.

Some theories and books about heaven attempt to be deeply philosophical and profound. To some it seems too easy to place humans on a real earth where they will have real bodies, but God chose the earth as the perfect place for us in the beginning. Though it is only a remnant of what it once was, it is still incredibly beautiful. Truly, God created it as a perfect paradise for us because, even in its cursed, dying state, it beams of majesty and splendor.

We can have a very good idea of what the New Earth will be like because the Bible tells us about the earth before sin's contamination (Genesis 1 and 2). The New Earth will be a restoration of the current earth to the paradise of God's original plan, and according to Revelation 21, he will make his home here with us when that happens.

If you still aren't convinced that this earth will be the location of our heavenly reward, consider once more what Peter wrote in Acts 3:21: "He [Jesus] must remain in heaven until the time comes for God to restore everything, as he promised long ago through his holy prophets."

Note that this passage says God will restore *everything*. Because we have never lived in a disembodied, otherworldly state, for God to take us to such a place would not qualify as a restoration at all. When a painting or a car is restored, it is made to resemble its original design before the decay. The original characteristics are brought back and the damage is removed. If someone attempted to restore Leonardo da Vinci's painting of Mona Lisa but turned it into a painting that looked like Vincent Van Gogh's "Starry Night," we would not consider that a restoration. Or if we hired an expert auto mechanic to restore our 1965 Ford Mustang and he came back with a car that looked like a 1962 Chevrolet Impala, we would know that he had not performed a restoration.

The reward in the next life for Christians is God restoring the earth, humans, and the entire physical universe to his original design.

Peter not only learned of the restoration concept through the prophets, he heard it from Jesus himself. When Peter told Jesus that the disciples had left everything to follow him, he wanted a reward or a pat on the back from Jesus. Jesus didn't scold or rebuke him but said: "I tell you the truth, at the renewal of all things, when the Son of Man sits on his glorious throne, you who have followed me will also sit on twelve thrones, judging the twelve tribes of Israel" (Matthew 19:27-28).

Did you notice the Lord's choice of words? He didn't say "at the annihilation of all things" or "at the departure of all things" but "at the *renewal* of all things."

When we renew something, we make it as it was in the beginning. When we renew a contract, we reaffirm the original agreement. When a married couple renews their vows, they rekindle their original dedication to each other. If a married couple sent you an invitation to their vow-renewal ceremony and they made vows to other people, you certainly wouldn't call that a *renewal* of their vows would you?

Christ's statement in Matthew 19:27-28 distinguishes between two deeply different theologies. God created humans to live on the earth. That is what Christ guaranteed at his resurrection—a renewed humanity on a renewed earth with a renewed relationship with God. The belief that the heaven God plans for us will be unearthly and non-human is not the biblical picture. God made the earth for us to live on and made us to live on the earth. God ransomed his creation; he didn't go back to the drawing board. That is why it is called redemption.

As Anthony Hoekema writes, "If God would have to annihilate the present cosmos, Satan would have won a great victory . . . . Satan would have succeeded in so devastatingly corrupting the present cosmos and the present earth that God could do nothing with it but to blot it totally out of existence. But Satan did not win such a victory. On the contrary, Satan has been decisively defeated. God will reveal the full dimensions of that defeat when He shall renew this very earth on which Satan deceived mankind and finally banish from it all the results of Satan's evil machinations." [*The Bible and the Future* (Grand Rapids: Eerdmans, 1979), 280]

Is This My Father's World?

I believe that one of the reasons some Christians have difficulty understanding that heaven will actually be on earth is because of their interpretation of passages that tell us to distance ourselves from the world.

John wrote, "Do not love the world or anything in the world" (1 John 2:15), and yet he also wrote, "For God so loved the world that he gave his one and only Son" (John 3:16). James echoes John's call to defy the world: "Don't you know that friendship with the world is hatred toward God? Anyone who chooses to be a friend of the world becomes an enemy of God" (James 4:4). John makes an even more definitive statement about the world: "We know that we are children of God, and that the whole world is under the control of the evil one" (I John 5:19).

How can Jesus love it but we are told not to? How can he love the world when it is under the control of the evil one? As with most words, context determines meaning. The world tied to Satan is the system or order of things related to the fall and God's casting him out of heaven. The world that Jesus loves is one that we may love as well. God's creation. God's people living on that creation. We must not love the things that are related to the fall that John allies with his use of the word "world": "For everything in the world—the cravings of sinful man, the lust of his eyes and the boasting of what he has and does—comes not from the Father but from the world. The world and its desires pass away, but the man who does the will of God lives forever" (1 John 2:16-17). He writes that those things are not from the Father. But this earth is. He created it. I don't love the world that John warns about, but I readily admit I love the earth that God made. How can we not love a world that God created for us?

I intensely dislike what has happened to the world because of the fall, but I love the creation God made for us. I long for the curse to be gone and the earth to be whole as it once was.

Compare our feelings about this fallen earth to the citizens of the former communist Russia. Those who wanted change both loved and hated their country. They hated it because of the restrictive, life-controlling government that persecuted so many. However, it was their motherland and they loved it. Not the corruption that defiled it, but the land that was their home. It was that love that propelled the people of Russia to defy the communist-controlled Soviets and bring about change. In the same way, we are to defy the earth *in its present form* because we know that God originally made it to be a much better place than it is now. But contrary to the song I learned as a child, this world *is* my home. I'm not just passing through. My treasures aren't laid up somewhere beyond the blue. I will live on the New Earth for an eternity and my treasures will be here where God sets up his heavenly kingdom.

We don't reject the earth God created; we reject what goes against God, not only to bring glory to God out of the ashes of this fallen world, but also to bring glory to God in the New Earth by bringing as many with us as possible.

There Is Much to Be Done in Heaven

I know a very wealthy man who recently re-entered the job market. He had retired in his mid-thirties with more money than most people will see in a lifetime. Nevertheless, he wanted to return to work.

Are you thinking, "The man couldn't take a life of having anything he wanted and getting to sleep late every day?!" I sheepishly admit that at first I did. As I began to have more and more contact with him, I realized that he lived with the demeanor of a man on a permanent vacation. He didn't seem to show the stress of running a business or staying up late to finish projects. He smiled easily and was anxious to roll his sleeves up and take on new projects. At first, I thought he returned to work in order to build more wealth, but I slowly realized that he worked because he enjoyed working. His life exemplified a principle of human nature that we sometimes forget—the desire to be productive.

We all want to accomplish something worthwhile. If we are not enthusiastic about accomplishing things at our job, it's likely because we're wishing we were somewhere else doing something else. On the other hand, if we are doing something that interests us and provides us with a sense of satisfaction when we are finished, we experience a joy God programmed into us.

God created human beings to work, to be productive, and to accomplish goals.

God did not separate work from paradise. He created the Garden of Eden as a paradise, yet required work from Adam and Eve. "The LORD God took the man and put him in the Garden of Eden to work it and take care of it" (Genesis 2:15).

When God restores the earth, we'll work, but it won't be like the work we do now. Because of the curse, work became frustrating and repetitive at times. "God said, 'Cursed is the ground because of you; through painful toil you will eat of it all the days of your life. It will produce thorns and thistles for you, and you will eat the plants of the field. By the sweat of your brow you will eat your food"' (Genesis 3:17-19). Work on the New Earth will not be such unsatisfying drudgery or wasted hours. "No longer will there be any curse. The throne of God and of the Lamb will be in the city and his servants will serve him" (Revelation 22:3).

What Will We Do on the New Earth?

As we read a few paragraphs above, God gave Adam the responsibility of working and taking care of the Garden of Eden. He also made Adam responsible for subduing the earth and ruling (shepherding) the animals: ". . . fill the earth and subdue it. Rule over the fish of the sea and the birds of the air and over every living creature that moves on the ground.' Then God said, 'I give you every seed-bearing plant on the face of the whole earth and every tree that has fruit with seed in it. They will be yours for food"' (Genesis 1:28-29).

God gave humankind a world to live in and required humankind to be responsible for that world. Humans would plant seeds, harvest crops, tend the animals, and do all the other things required as caretakers of the earth. So will it be on the New Earth. We will care for the New Earth and all who inhabit it. There won't be need for hospitals because of our incorruptible resurrection bodies, but I believe there will be places for schools and learning, as well as ways to serve each other. After all, someone has to mow the greens so that some of us can play golf! (I guess that means others will be making clubs, others teaching golf, and yet others consoling the golfers who lose.)

Will Everything Go Our Way on the New Earth?

Will we experience frustrations on the New Earth? Not to the degree that we have them on this current earth but, yes, I think there will be times when things don't always go our way. But not to the extent that we're worried our children won't eat or that a health problem is going to take the life of someone we love.

Occasional frustrations and failures are part of the human experience. What fun would sports be if every team always won no matter what effort level they put into preparation for the game? "Do not be deceived: God cannot be mocked. A man reaps what he sows" (Galatians 6:7). God's laws still hold true on the New Earth. As we discussed previously, we will be productive on the New Earth. We'll be working and sometimes we'll achieve all of our goals and sometimes maybe we won't. Working smart, hard, and consistently will still count.

Being a morally perfect human will be our nature, but that doesn't mean we can do every physical task we set out to perfectly. Being holy doesn't mean that we can all slam dunk basketballs, write beautiful poetry, be a convincing actor, or have a knack for repairing engines. Being holy means that we don't break God's laws and that we have fellowship with him; it doesn't mean that we'll all be star athletes or geniuses.

We'll still have challenges, less than perfect decisions, incorrect assumptions, and deadlines. But we'll handle them all so much better than in this present life. We'll still have adventures, near misses, and alarm clocks. We'll still occasionally feel tired from working and need to go to bed early. Yes, I believe we will still sleep on the New Earth. Rest, after all, is a human experience that's beneficial emotionally, spiritually, mentally, and physically. It's a pleasurable experience and there's nothing unholy about sleep or the way the human body works. God created our bodies to work in the amazing ways they do. The fall robbed us of living in bodies that functioned correctly, but our bodies still function using many of the amazing and complex systems God put within them.

The New Earth will give us human life to the fullest where we can have fellowship with God, the angels, and each other. Many of our present daily activities will still be part of life on the New Earth. Sin and death will be eliminated and we'll get to see what God had in mind for us in the beginning.

Will We Compete? Will We Have Hobbies and Fun?

I recall a conversation with a Christian who informed several of us that there would be no competition in heaven and thus no sports of any kind. He based his belief on 1 John 2:15 that tells us not to love the world. He claimed that playing sports was showing love for the world. This man went on to say that not only would there not be sports in heaven, but that playing sports in this life was a sin.

Many of us were taken aback by his claims and weren't sure what to say, but finally a few of us raised some interesting questions for him. We asked if he had any hobbies at all such as watching television, reading a book, playing an occasional video game, watching a movie, going out to eat with friends, playing charades, going on vacations, surfing the Internet, playing a musical instrument, listening to someone else play musical instruments, looking at paintings, scanning through a magazine, telling jokes, taking walks, and several other things that most humans do for enjoyment and amusement.

He confessed to a few of those and added gardening and exercise. I've since forgotten how he justified his hobbies, but he insisted that those of us who enjoyed watching a football game or playing in a softball game were sinning because it was "of the world." He held the mistaken idea that enjoying something is somehow less spiritual than sitting in a chair solemnly contemplating life or quietly meditating.

God created humans with certain capacities. We can love, enjoy, laugh, feel sorrow, feel guilt, be angry (but sin not says Ephesians 4:26), be lonely, have fun, be excited, and all kinds of other combinations of emotions and feelings. If God created us with these capacities, how could they be sinful or "less spiritual?" Are we to assume that Jesus never laughed or did anything purely for the enjoyment of it? Did he not tell an occasional joke? Did he not play any of the games that other young Jewish children played?

The Bible tells us the kinds of attributes we should see in those who have surrendered their lives to God. The Bible calls those attributes "fruits of the Spirit." Here's the list: "But the fruit of the Spirit is love, joy, peace, patience, kindness, goodness, faithfulness, gentleness and self-control" (Galatians 5:22-23). Notice that joy is listed among the attributes we should see in our Christian brothers and sisters. God created us to feel joy and to experience things in life that bring us joy. Remember, God's command to Adam and Eve was that they not eat of the Tree of Knowledge of Good and Evil. He didn't command them to be slaves to solitude or sticks in the mud.

The Bible often tells us of people rejoicing and being joyful, going to feasts and anticipating celebrations and parties. Here are a few examples:

They ate and drank with great joy in the presence of the LORD that day. Then they acknowledged Solomon son of David as king a second time, anointing him before the LORD to be ruler and Zadok to be priest. (1 Chronicles 29:22)

Then, led by Jehoshaphat, all the men of Judah and Jerusalem returned joyfully to Jerusalem, for the Lord had given them cause to rejoice over their enemies. (2 Chronicles 20:27)

Nehemiah said, "Go and enjoy choice food and sweet drinks, and send some to those who have nothing prepared. This day is sacred to our Lord. Do not grieve, for the joy of the LORD is your strength." (Nehemiah 8:10)

In every province and in every city, wherever the edict of the king went, there was joy and gladness among the Jews, with feasting and celebrating. (Esther 8:17)

He will yet fill your mouth with laughter and your lips with shouts of joy. (Job 8:21)

You turned my wailing into dancing; you removed my sackcloth and clothed me with joy . . . . (Psalm 30:10-12)

This list could grow quite large, so we'll stop there with the basic point
that feeling joy, celebrating, and sharing joy with others is a wonderful
thing that is mentioned many times in the Bible.

When Jesus told parables about the kingdom of heaven, he would
often use a feast or celebration to describe it.

Jesus spoke to them again in parables, saying: "The kingdom
of heaven is like a king who prepared a wedding banquet for
his son. He sent his servants to those who had been invited to
the banquet to tell them to come, but they refused to come.

"Then he sent some more servants and said, 'Tell those
who have been invited that I have prepared my dinner: My
oxen and fattened cattle have been butchered, and everything
is ready. Come to the wedding banquet.'

"But they paid no attention and went off—one to his field,
another to his business. The rest seized his servants, mistreated them and killed them. The king was enraged. He sent his
army and destroyed those murderers and burned their city.

"Then he said to his servants, 'The wedding banquet is
ready, but those I invited did not deserve to come. Go to the
street corners and invite to the banquet anyone you find.' So
the servants went out into the streets and gathered all the

people they could find, both good and bad, and the wedding hall was filled with guests." (Matthew 22:1-10)

Jesus used a banquet celebration to describe the kingdom of heaven. And then later, when an angel is speaking to John while he is writing the book of Revelation, we read of the angel telling him: "'Blessed are those who are invited to the wedding supper of the Lamb!'" And he added, "These are the true words of God" (Revelation 19:9).

Jesus told us that there would be many who would come from all over the earth and would feast with Abraham, Isaac, and Jacob in heaven on the New Earth (Matthew 8:11 and see Luke 22:29-30). The point here is that God can also feel joy and celebrate and wants us to do the same. His kingdom will be a place where we can share in his joy. We can celebrate and play. We'll work and accomplish things but we'll also experience rest, relaxation, and fun (Revelation 14:13).

I can imagine softball games, rounds of golf, flag football, throwing the baseball around, tossing a Frisbee in the park, and hikes in the mountains. Heaven on the New Earth will be a place where we don't experience death or sin. Many if not most of the other things we experience in this life will be part of life on the New Earth. I don't see why there wouldn't be books, modes of transportation, computers, telephones, stores, roads, televisions, movie theaters, restaurants, birthday parties, card games, and picnics. Why wouldn't there be? Are we sinning now when we are doing or using those things?

I can tell you that on the New Earth you won't see or use hospitals, drug stores, funeral homes, or cemeteries. But let's not lump human advances in technology, fun activities, or productivity in with things that are inherently sinful. The restoration of all things (Acts 3:21) brings the removal of the bad and the return to what is good. We'll still enjoy the wholesome things God created us to enjoy and we'll still learn more about how to do things better and apply knowledge.

We Will Serve Him by Ruling with Him.

That may sound odd because it is not something Christians typically talk about, especially in public. It's not a popular topic from the pulpit. It sounds far too politically incorrect to say, "One day Christians will rule the earth with God." It might not be politically correct, but the Bible tells us that it will happen. Just as humans were to rule the original earth (as shown in passages above), humans will participate in ruling the New Earth.

"Do you not know that the saints will judge the world? And if you are to judge the world, are you not competent to judge trivial cases? Do you not know that we will judge angels?" (1 Corinthians 6:2)

"[I]f we endure, we will also reign with him." (2 Timothy 2:12)

"To him who overcomes, I will give the right to sit with me on my throne, just as I overcame and sat down with my Father on his throne." (Revelation 3:21)

On the New Earth, God will be the King and we will be his royal servants. We also will rule with him as active participants in his kingdom. God's children will carry out what he first appointed Adam and Eve to do: "They will reign forever and ever" (Revelation 22:5).

We will reign with God in his kingdom. It might sound extreme, but it's been in the Bible all along.

> "Then the King will say to those on his right, 'Come, you who are blessed by my Father; take your inheritance, the kingdom prepared for you since the creation of the world.'" (Matthew 25:34)

> "Blessed are the meek, for they will inherit the earth." (Matthew 5:5)

> "Be faithful, even to the point of death, and I will give you the crown of life." (Revelation 2:10)

> "[Y]ou have redeemed us to God by Your blood out of every tribe and tongue and people and nation, and have made us kings and priests to our God; and we shall reign on the earth." (Revelation 5:9-10, NKJV)

We will be kings and priests, but how and what will we do in those positions? The Bible is not as clear as I wish it would be. It's a little easier to understand the way that some people will rule. When Peter asked what the apostles would get in return for leaving everything for

Jesus, Jesus replied: "I tell you the truth, at the renewal of all things, when the Son of Man sits on his glorious throne, you who have followed me will also sit on twelve thrones, judging the twelve tribes of Israel" (Matthew 19:28).

Will some of us rule towns, cities, states, even countries on the New Earth? Will we be responsible for the care and upkeep of certain areas and lands, some of which we may actually own? I don't know for sure, but if God promised us that we will reign, then we shall reign.

We won't be stale, mindless robots in heaven but, as already mentioned, will keep our personalities and idiosyncrasies. Just as God uses our giftedness here to serve his kingdom in different ways, it appears God will use our giftedness in the New Earth to serve his kingdom, especially in serving others. Some of us were gifted to take charge of certain aspects of a venture, while others were more gifted in carrying out the details of missions and projects. Remember, even in heaven the clay does not question its Potter (Isaiah 45:9). God will still be God no matter how great our level of responsibility or reward.

Levels of Reward

Sometimes people ask if hell will be worse for some and heaven better for some. Both appear to be true. Here is a passage about judgment for those who will be punished:

Then Jesus began to denounce the cities in which most of his miracles had been performed, because they did not repent.

"Woe to you, Korazin! Woe to you, Bethsaida! If the miracles that were performed in you had been performed in Tyre and Sidon, they would have repented long ago in sackcloth and ashes. But I tell you, it will be more bearable for Tyre and Sidon on the day of judgment than for you. And you, Capernaum, will you be lifted up to the skies? No, you will go down to the depths. If the miracles that were performed in you had been performed in Sodom, it would have remained to this day. But I tell you that it will be more bearable for Sodom on the day of judgment than for you." (Matthew 11:20-24)

I don't know all that is implied about judgment being more bearable for some than others, but the gist of Jesus' teaching here is frightening. Certain people will fare worse than others.

Some judgment will be more severe, but any judgment that leads to punishment is absolutely awful.

If we deliberately keep on sinning after we have received the knowledge of the truth, no sacrifice for sins is left, but only a fearful expectation of judgment and of raging fire that will consume the enemies of God. Anyone who rejected the law of Moses died without mercy on the testimony of two or three witnesses. How much more severely do you think a man deserves to be punished who has trampled the Son of God under foot, who has treated as an unholy thing the blood of the covenant that sanctified him, and who has insulted the Spirit of grace? For we know him who said, "It is mine to avenge; I will repay," and again, "The Lord will judge his people." It is a dreadful thing to fall into the hands of the living God. (Hebrews 10:26-31)

When it comes to heaven, the Bible tells us there are also levels or degrees of reward.

The man who plants and the man who waters have one purpose, and each will be rewarded according to his own labor. For we are God's fellow workers; you are God's field, God's building.

By the grace God has given me, I laid a foundation as an expert builder, and someone else is building on it. But each one should be careful how he builds. For no one can lay any foundation other than the one already laid, which is Jesus Christ. If any man builds on this foundation using gold, silver, costly stones, wood, hay or straw, his work will be shown for what it is, because the Day will bring it to light. It will be revealed with fire, and the fire will test the quality of each man's work. If what he has built survives, he will receive his reward. (1 Corinthians 3:8-14)

We cannot earn our salvation; it is by grace through faith, not by works so that no one can boast (Ephesians 2:9). However, the treasures laid up for us in heaven have to do with our service to God here before death. In the passage above, Paul indicates that we receive rewards based on the validity of what we have done to build the kingdom of God. Things we did that turn out not to be of quality will be "burned" away. No reward for those. Things we did that aided the kingdom will be rewarded each according to his own labor.

Jesus told a rich young man to sell his possessions and give the money to the poor "and you will have treasure in heaven" (Matthew 19:21). Paul said that rich folks who were generous laid up for themselves treasures in heaven.

> Command those who are rich in this present world not to be arrogant nor to put their hope in wealth, which is so uncertain, but to put their hope in God, who richly provides us with everything for our enjoyment. Command them to do good, to be rich in good deeds, and to be generous and willing to share. In this way they will lay up treasure for themselves as a firm foundation for the coming age, so that they may take hold of the life that is truly life. (1 Timothy 6:17-19)

God keeps count of our selflessness and our taking care of our fellow man. Quite literally, we receive a reward in heaven for those good deeds. Salvation is free. Rewards are consequences for doing right. John quotes Jesus in Revelation 22:12 as saying: "Behold, I am coming soon! My reward is with me, and I will give to everyone according to what he has done."

Fellow students confronted one of my high-school Bible teachers about these passages, and to this day I appreciate his reply. He said, "I'll be happy even if I have the last spot on the *floor* to sit." However, we should do our best to honor God by striving to be "called great" in his kingdom. If rewarding us individually didn't matter to God, he wouldn't have provided incentives for doing good things and striving to honor him in all we do.

Again, let me repeat: being rewarded for good works and salvation are two different things. Salvation is by grace through faith and we can't ever do enough good works to earn or deserve it. The Bible is clear about that. But the Bible is also clear when it tells us that we will receive rewards for our actions.

Okay, This May Sound Weird, But . . . .

We live on one planet in a gigantic universe containing an uncountable number of other planets and stars that are the result of God's endless creativity. You don't need the Hubble Telescope to tell you that, though many of the pictures of galaxies extraordinary distances from earth fascinate and intrigue us. Just step outside and look to the stars.

Why does the Bible tell us that we will not only receive a New Earth, but a new universe? How very interesting! What would be the point of having a new universe with all that space just sitting there idle? I hope that in the new bodies in the renewed creation, humans can be involved in projects in other realms of the universe other than just the New Earth. It's *all* his after all.

When we consider God's incredibly large creation and his endless capacity to create, we can also see that the possibility for adventure, exploration, and learning are just as endless.

Will Animals Be in Heaven?

I cried as I helped my brother dig the grave. I'd always hoped that "Ole Yeller" and "Turner and Hooch" would remain Hollywood stories and not part of real life.

Bullet was a boxer bulldog with a personality that attracted love and attention. He didn't have a temper and enjoyed being with the four humans who made him part of their family. It might sound silly, but his collar had a metal tag that included our last name after his. We had many adventures together, and a boy couldn't have asked for a more loyal friend. I miss him to this day.

I'd always been taught that because dogs didn't have souls, they didn't go to heaven when they died. They simply returned to the dust and completely ceased to exist, except within the memories of those who loved them. When we buried Bullet part of the pain was believing that he would never exist again.

Later I fell in love with a much smaller dog. Bo was smaller only in stature, not spirit or pride. He was a beautiful, miniature long-haired dachshund that embodied the saying, "You're only as big as you think you are." Bo thought he was a Saint Bernard.

On steroids.

One of my fondest memories of Bo is an incident that happened while walking through a Georgia neighborhood on a fall afternoon. Bo always strutted with his head up, as regal as any king and as confident as any supermodel. He was proud, but kind. As we walked through the neighborhood, he barked at much bigger dogs to remind them that he tolerated them in his world, not the other way around.

Most of the other dogs didn't react. They knew the only way he could hurt them was if they choked on him. Unfortunately, this particular day Bo didn't get the usual dismissal. As we walked by a large dog that appeared to be a Doberman mix, Bo started his noisy routine.

The dog leapt to his feet and charged.

Bo let out a high-pitched yelp and literally jumped up into my arms. Never before or after did Bo ever come close to jumping that high, but he made the leap of a lifetime that day. The behemoth circled us several times, barking at Bo, who continued to bark right back from the safety of his perch atop my shoulders. (Yes, he actually climbed from my arms to my shoulders.) Finally, the dog walked away. When he reached a safe distance, I put Bo down. He walked on as proud as he always did, except for a slight wobble in his knees.

A few years after that walk, Bo chased a wild duck into the street. He never saw the car.

How terribly depressing it would be for the story to end there, and for years I thought it did. Yet, as I began to study what the Bible says about heaven and the New Earth, I realized that those who taught me that animals were left out of heaven were making assumptions. Quite simply, if God created animals to live in his ideal world (the Garden of Eden), why would God not have animals on the New Earth?

Biblical Imagery of Animals Beyond This World

Though I was taught there would be no animals in heaven, God sent an amazing type of horse to take Elijah to heaven.

As they were walking along and talking together, suddenly a chariot of fire and horses of fire appeared and separated the two of them, and Elijah went up to heaven in a whirlwind. Elisha saw this and cried out, "My father! My father! The chariots and horsemen of Israel!" And Elisha saw him no more. Then he took hold of his own clothes and tore them apart (2 Kings 2:11-12)

Later Elisha found himself surrounded by an enemy army with horses and chariots. He did not fear because of what he could see that they couldn't.

When the servant of the man of God got up and went out early the next morning, an army with horses and chariots had surrounded the city. "Oh, my lord, what shall we do?" the servant asked. "Don't be afraid," the prophet answered. "Those who are with us are more than those who are with them." And Elisha prayed, "O LORD, open his eyes so he may see." Then the LORD opened the servant's eyes, and he looked and saw the hills full of horses and chariots of fire all around Elisha. (2 Kings 6:15-17)

Several times in Revelation John refers to horses in heaven. Other animals mentioned in heaven, such as the four living creatures, are extraordinary beings that apparently aren't human or angel (Revelation 4:6; 7:11, and others).

I look forward to a time such as Isaiah described: "The wolf and the lamb will feed together and the lion will eat straw like the ox .... They will neither harm nor destroy on all my holy mountain" (Isaiah 65:25).

Things Were Different for Animals at First.

In the beginning, God created animals to live on the earth. Apparently humans and animals were vegetarians in the Garden of Eden. God said that he gave all animals plants to eat. "'And to all the beasts of the earth and all the birds of the air and all the creatures that move on the ground—everything that has the breath of life in it—I give every green plant for food.' And it was so" (Genesis 1:30). After the flood things were different:

Then God blessed Noah and his sons, saying to them, "Be fruitful and increase in number and fill the earth. The fear and dread of you will fall upon all the beasts of the earth and all the birds of the air, upon every creature that moves along the ground, and upon all the fish of the sea; they are given into your hands. Everything that lives and moves will be food for you. Just as I gave you the green plants, I now give you everything." (Genesis 9:1-3)

I have difficulty imagining a bulldog tearing into a big piece of broccoli, but if before the fall animals all ate plants, then after the renewal they could do so again.

All of Creation Awaits the Renewal.

Consider the words of Romans 8:19-22:

The creation waits in eager expectation for the sons of God to be revealed. For the creation was subjected to frustration, not by its own choice, but by the will of the one who subjected it, in hope that the creation itself will be liberated from its bondage to decay and brought into the glorious freedom of the children of God. We know that the whole creation has been groaning as in the pains of childbirth right up to the present time.

Because the leader of the earth (Adam) fell, all creation fell along with him. The Bible tells us that God will restore all creation, not just man. After all, it's all his. "God made the wild animals according to their kinds, the livestock according to their kinds, and all the creatures that move along the ground according to their kinds. And God saw that it was good" (Genesis 1:25). God put animals on the original earth and said it was good. Why would they not be there when God restores the original to all its glory? If God is going to put humans back on the New Earth, why wouldn't he place animals there as well?

Do Animals Have Souls?

Whether or not animals have souls is irrelevant to their existence on the New Earth. God could easily recreate animals on the New Earth with or without souls. However, for the sake of our study consider the following passage: "[T]he Lord God formed the man from the dust of the ground and breathed into his nostrils the breath of life, and the man became a living being" (Genesis 2:7).

The King James Version translates "living being" as "living soul," and man wasn't a "living soul" until God "breathed into his nostrils the breath of life." The Hebrew word is *nephesh*, and God breathed it into animals as well: "And to all the beasts of the earth and all the birds of the air and all the creatures that move on the ground—everything that has the breath of life in it . . ." (Genesis 1:30).

You see, when God breathed *nephesh* into Adam, Adam became *nephesh*. According to the Bible, God also breathed *nephesh* into the animals. Other passages that use this word concerning animals are Genesis 6:17, where the NIV translates it as "the breath of life": "I am going to bring floodwaters on the earth to destroy all life under the heavens, every creature that has the breath of life in it. Everything on earth will perish." And the translation of *nephesh* in Genesis 7:15 follows suit: "Pairs of all creatures that have the breath of life in them came to Noah and entered the ark."

The concept of the soul as we generally know it came later in history. In the Old Testament people didn't think of themselves as spirits living in a body as we typically do. They thought of themselves as the outer person (the one others see) and the inner person (who one really is on the inside). While they had a concept of ghosts and necromancy, the nuances were not the same as ours. To them, body and soul were part and parcel of the same thing. For example, Vine says regarding the word *nephesh*:

> The Hebrew system of thought does not include the combination or opposition of the terms "body" and "soul," which are really Greek and Latin in origin. The Hebrew contrasts two other concepts which are not found in the Greek and Latin tradition: "the inner self" and "the outer appearance" or, as viewed in a different context, "what one is to oneself" as opposed to "what one appears to be to one's observers." [*Vine's Complete Expository Dictionary of Old and New Testament Words* (1985), 237-238]

To think of humans as spirits and animals as not spirits doesn't really fit into the concept of *nephesh*. God made our bodies and he

157

made theirs. They are not the same as us in some ways but are the same as us in many ways. We have a different level of intellect, of course, but much of what God put into them (DNA similarities, certain drives and needs, etc.) he also put into human beings.

Don't put me in a pigeonhole here. I had a chicken sandwich for lunch and had roast beef for dinner last night. I wouldn't hesitate to sacrifice any animal to prevent damage to a human. (Watch out squirrels.) My point isn't that animals are equal to humans, but that God made them just as carefully as he made humans. He put them on this earth before he put us here. He made them *nephesh* as he did us. We are to rule them, but they are his creation also and matter to him.

A Covenant with Animals?

If you're still not convinced that God cares for animals and sees them as an important part of earth, consider the story of the great flood. Noah was to take representatives of all kinds of animals with him so that they wouldn't die out.

Perhaps the most interesting part of this story is that God made the post-flood covenant not only with man, but with the animals as well. "Then God said to Noah and to his sons with him: 'I now establish my covenant with you and your descendants after you and with every living creature that was with you—the birds, the livestock and all the wild animals, all those that came out of the ark with you—every living creature on earth'" (Genesis 9:8-10).

Not only did God add animals to this covenant, but when he purified the earth with the flood, and, in a sense, renewed it, God's plan for earth *still* included animals. He made sure that Noah had two of each so that animals would continue to populate the earth.

Just as God had them on the renewed earth then, I believe God will have them on the eternal New Earth of the future.

We Are to Care for God's Animals

A large part of our duty as humans is to take care of and rule over earth's animals. God told humans to "rule over the fish of the sea and the birds of the air and over every living creature that moves on the ground" (Genesis 1:28).

Though we care for and rule over the animals, they ultimately belong to God: "[F]or every animal of the forest is mine, and the cattle on a thousand hills. I know every bird in the mountains, and the creatures of the field are mine" (Psalm 50:10-11).

Ruling over animals means a variety of things, including being able to eat them (Genesis 9:3). Though at times most humans use certain animals for food, God instilled within humanity a sense of responsibility for them. Proverbs 12:10 says, "The righteous care for the needs of their animals . . . ." Even in our increasingly secular-minded world, we have laws against cruelty to animals. Somehow, we know that animals should not be mistreated and that we should provide them some sort of defense against harm.

It's a complicated balance that will not exist on the New Earth because death will be no more. As it appears was the case in the Garden of Eden, it seems there will be no meat eaters on the New Earth. Therefore, we probably will not use animals as a source of food. However, if God allows, I'd still love a good steak now and then.

God Made Animals for Our Company

As most of us remember from the story of the Garden of Eden, God had Adam name all the animals, and during this process he learned that none was a suitable helper for him. He learned them, watched them, and figured out names for them based on their behavior. It is within us to enjoy their company and share life with them. Every pet owner knows that very well.

Just as God made angels different from humans, he made humans different from animals. He designed all of his creatures to function and interact with each other in the beginning, and he will restore that fellowship on the New Earth.

I'm convinced that death has not stolen our lost pets forever, just as it has not stolen our family members and friends who have passed away. God's plan is to reunite all of his creation again on the New Earth. He tells us that he will reconcile *all* things to himself.

For by him all things were created: things in heaven and on earth, visible and invisible, whether thrones or powers or rulers or authorities; all things were created by him and for

him. He is before all things, and in him all things hold together. And he is the head of the body, the church; he is the
beginning and the firstborn from among the dead, so that
in everything he might have the supremacy. For God was
pleased to have all his fullness dwell in him, and through him
to reconcile to himself all things, whether things on earth or
things in heaven, by making peace through his blood, shed on
the cross. (Colossians 1:16-20)

Admittedly, none of these passages indicates that God will specifically recreate Bo or Bullet. However, as Billy Graham wrote years ago
in his column in answer to a little girl's question about her deceased
pet, if God wants to make that pet for her again, he certainly has the
power and ability to do it. I have no doubt animals will be on the New
Earth. I'm asking that Bo and Bullet be among them.

Though we are different from the animal kingdom, we share similarities with them, the most important of which is that God created us
both and will redeem us both.

CHAPTER 9
Will We Still Be Male and Female?

After speaking about heaven at a church, I received a question that I'm asked occasionally but is likely rarely discussed in Bible classes around the world: "You said we retain our personalities and memories in heaven. Will my wife and I still be husband and wife? My wife says that if we can't share a 'mansion just over the hilltop,' can we at least get ones next door to each other?"

To answer, let's start back at the beginning.

Adam and Eve had a unique relationship. During their arguments or any times they felt they didn't want to be together, they likely returned to one central thought: "This person was created for me." In a very true sense, they completed each other. Before Eve's existence, Adam walked this earth devoid of another like him. Though God was with him, it was God himself who referred to Adam as being "alone" and said it was "not good" (Genesis 2:18).

When God required Adam to name the animals, he demonstrated to Adam that, like the other creatures on earth, he needed a companion. As with those other creatures, he had made, God created Eve to be more than Adam's company; God made her to be his lover. Together they would bring children to the earth.

God masterminded a coming together of a man and woman long before writers penned it or Hollywood filmed it. God designed the bodies of men and women to fit together when making love. He gave humankind the capacity to feel wonderful things physically, emotionally, and spiritually as they sexually bond.

Unfortunately, it isn't always viewed that way. I can tell you from my work in the area of sexology that many people are taught from a young age that our sexual urges are evil and that sex in general is a bad thing. Throughout adolescence teens hear that sex is bad and then just before they marry the message is changed to sex is good. When for years one has heard only about how bad it is, it's difficult to simply "flick the switch" and start seeing sex as something good. I often hear from people who actually feel guilty about making love with their spouses because they were taught for so many years that they shouldn't do that.

I urge parents to teach their children that sex is a wonderful blessing from God that is to be shared in a marriage relationship. Don't frame sex as something evil or twisted, but something wholesome and good when experienced in marriage.

Neither Married Nor Given in Marriage

You may be familiar with the story found both in Matthew and Mark in which a Sadducee thinks he can trip Jesus up about the belief in a resurrection of the dead. (Sadducees believed this life is all there is.)

That same day the Sadducees, who say there is no resurrection, came to him with a question. "Teacher," they said, "Moses told us that if a man dies without having children, his brother must marry the widow and have children for him. Now there were seven brothers among us. The first one married and died, and since he had no children, he left his wife to his brother. The same thing happened to the second and third brother, right on down to the seventh. Finally, the woman died. Now then, at the resurrection, whose wife will she be of the seven, since all of them were married to her?"

Jesus replied, "You are in error because you do not know the Scriptures or the power of God. At the resurrection people will neither marry nor be given in marriage; they will be like the angels in heaven. But about the resurrection of the dead—have you not read what God said to you, 'I am the God of Abraham, the God of Isaac, and the God of Jacob'? He is not the God of the dead but of the living."

When the crowds heard this, they were astonished at his teaching. (Matthew 22:23-33)

Let me remind you that the comparison to angels is limited to the fact that we, like the angels, will "neither marry nor be given in marriage." This verse is not saying that humans become angels after death.

What does the passage teach about marriage?

The answer to that question varies by groups within Christianity as well as by individual Bible scholars. The rank and file of those who call themselves Christian seem to hold incompatible views that they seldom, if ever, question.

For example, at funerals we regularly tell the widow or widower, as well as children and other loved ones, that they will reunite with their relative in the next life. No one seems to question statements such as "Mom's gone on now to be with Dad. We'll see them at the resurrection." At funerals we often read Bible verses that indicate reunion, such as this one:

> Brothers, we do not want you to be ignorant about those who fall asleep, or to grieve like the rest of men, who have no hope. We believe that Jesus died and rose again and so we believe that God will bring with Jesus those who have fallen asleep in him. According to the Lord's own word, we tell you that we who are still alive, who are left till the coming of the Lord, will certainly not precede those who have fallen asleep. For the Lord himself will come down from heaven, with a loud command, with the voice of the archangel and with the trumpet call of God, and the dead in Christ will rise first. After that, we

who are still alive and are left will be caught up together with them in the clouds to meet the Lord in the air. And so we will be with the Lord forever. (1 Thessalonians 4:13-17)

Nevertheless, if we ask the same people—ministers, laypeople, whomever—who give such hope to those whose loved one died whether there will be a family structure there similar to what we have here, they likely will say no. Citing verses such as the ones from Matthew 22 above, they say that marriage will not exist. Therefore, they say that family structure similar to what we have here will not exist. After all, it's messy enough with all the step family difficulties that come now. Think of the poor woman who had been married to seven brothers. Which of them is waiting in heaven for her to pass on so that they can have that wonderful reunion?

We know that marriage ends at death and often cite that in marriage vows when we promise faithfulness to our soon-to-be spouse "until death do us part." The Bible also tells us that marriage ends at death.

A woman is bound to her husband as long as he lives. But if her husband dies, she is free to marry anyone she wishes, but he must belong to the Lord. (1 Corinthians 7:39)

Do you not know, brothers—for I am speaking to men who know the law—that the law has authority over a man only as long as he lives? For example, by law a married woman is bound to her husband as long as he is alive, but if her husband dies, she is released from the law of marriage. (Romans 7:1)

Therefore, most of us seemingly have no problem agreeing that there will not be marriage in heaven, but it leaves large holes in our other thoughts. Will Mom still be Mom? In heaven is she a unisex being or is she a woman with woman thoughts and feelings, woman memories, and a woman sense of self? After all, if I will still be me in heaven with all my declarative memories as discussed in a previous chapter, I expect to be a man. I don't know how to be a woman and I do not know how not to be a man. Also, my resurrection body comes from this body and this body is male. Being male is not for me just a matter of flesh that will some day cease to exist. It is quite literally who I am.

Adam and Eve were created male and female. If they had not sinned, they would have populated the original earth with males and females. They did even after the fall, of course, but my point is that humans would have lived forever in their original bodies, taking care of the earth, and having direct fellowship with God—all the while eternally remaining male and female.

When God restores all things (Acts 3:21), will he not restore humans as well? God made us male and female at the outset and if God is going to bring about a restoration of "all things," wouldn't that include restoring us to male and female human beings as he originally created us?

We can contemplate Jesus, our only example of the first fruits of the resurrection body. It seems clear that Jesus was male in his resurrection body or else others wouldn't have recognized him as the man known to them as Jesus. We read of no passages describing him as appearing unisex or not masculine. Jesus himself said in Luke 24:39, "It is I myself."

Consider the following passage describing events that took place shortly after Jesus' resurrection:

> Then the disciples went back to their homes, but Mary stood outside the tomb crying. As she wept, she bent over to look into the tomb and saw two angels in white, seated where Jesus' body had been, one at the head and the other at the foot.
>
> They asked her, "Woman, why are you crying?"
>
> "They have taken my Lord away," she said, "and I don't know where they have put him." At this, she turned around and saw Jesus standing there, but she did not realize that it was Jesus.
>
> "Woman," he said, "why are you crying? Who is it you are looking for?"
>
> Thinking he was the gardener, she said, "Sir, if you have carried him away, tell me where you have put him, and I will get him."
>
> Jesus said to her, "Mary."
>
> She turned toward him and cried out in Aramaic, "Rabboni!" (which means Teacher). (John 20:10-16)

Note that even before Mary knew it was Jesus, just a quick glance at him before she turned away told her that the person who stood nearby was a man. We know that because she called him "Sir." Then she recognized his voice saying her name and that's when she turned around and joyously called him "Teacher" and ran to embrace him. Had his voice not sounded masculine, as it would have in his life as a man, she would not have recognized the voice saying her name as the voice of Jesus.

When I used to view the next life as living as a disembodied spirit standing around the throne singing for eternity, thoughts like this one never came to mind. But when I realized that there will be a New Heaven and New Earth, populated with God's people in glorious resurrection bodies, these questions naturally began to arise.

I guess by now you've figured out that we will be male and female on the New Earth, as humans were male and female on the original earth before the fall of humankind.

The Legal Complexities of Marriage

Since we will be male and female on the New Earth, that creates another question. What was Jesus telling us when he said that we will neither marry nor be given in marriage after the resurrection?

We all interpret everything we come into contact with through the filter of what we already believe and have already experienced. That's human. Therefore, because the Bible emphasizes marriage over single people cohabitating as if they were married, it's easy to conclude that Jesus was saying that we wouldn't be male and female. Otherwise our minds start going to uncomfortable places with thoughts of still having gender but not being married, and that sounds a lot like sexual immorality. Therefore, we conclude that Jesus meant we become sexless or unisex beings.

But before rooting that in concrete, let's see if we can think of other possible meanings of Jesus' statement that we won't be married in heaven.

One, as we have already discussed, is that angels are unisex and have no need for marriage. Therefore, in the next life we will have the same condition. Another possibility could be that angels have gender but that they don't get married. In the next life we will have the same condition.

If we consider this second possibility, then we have to consider subheads. Subhead A is that, though they have gender, they do not have sexual relations. Therefore, they have no need of marriage. Subhead B is that they do have sexual relations of some sort, because they have gender, but not within the confines of marriage. Now that's definitely not in line with the beliefs that most Christians hold.

Marriage is a legal contract or recognition of commitment between two people. By marrying they gain the benefits of being considered as one unit and forego certain liberties that they had while single. As in the verses from 1 Corinthians and Romans 7 cited earlier, marriage has to do with law. Law governs marriage and when law ceases, the rules enjoined by that law no longer have effect. (For example, during prohibition liquor was illegal. Prohibition was repealed and liquor was no longer illegal.)

Adam and Eve didn't marry in the same legal sense that you or I would because there was no legal need. Because no other humans existed, there was no reason or boundaries to define what a couple was, and no reason to make a commitment that they would be only with each other. They didn't sin by not being legally married. They violated no law to live together. They were one in God's eyes and that's all that mattered because no other law existed.

The Hebrew word for wife, *ishshah*, is also the word for "woman" [William Gesenius, Francis Brown, S. R. Driver, and Charles Briggs, *A Hebrew and English Lexicon of the Old Testament* (Oxford, 1952)]. Translators of the Bible chose to use the English word "wife" in referring to Eve as "Adam's wife" in Genesis 2:25, but as easily could have used the word "woman" which would have simply called Eve, "Adam's woman." It's the same word that's translated as "woman" in Genesis 2:22, which says: "The Lord God fashioned into a woman the rib which he had taken from the man, and brought her to the man" (NASV).

The Hebrew word for a married woman or bride is *kallah*. It referred to a woman in either stage of Jewish marriage, either formally engaged or having already consummated the marriage. It is used in Isaiah 61:10, which says: "I delight greatly in the Lord; my soul rejoices in my God. For he has clothed me with garments of salvation and arrayed me in a robe of righteousness, as a bridegroom adorns his head like a priest and as a bride adorns herself with her jewels."

Before the population increased, it simply wasn't necessary to refer to Eve as a wife. She was a woman. The only woman. And that woman lived with the only man. We can call it marriage because of its intent and effect, but legally no marriage was needed.

Interestingly, as the law did come into effect, there are biblical situations that are hard to understand or explain. In 1 Kings 11:3 we read about King Solomon having seven hundred wives! He also had three hundred concubines. Concubines were female companions of Solomon with whom he could have sexual relations and through whom he could father children. Solomon's father was King David whom 1 Samuel 13:14 calls a man after God's own heart. Michal was David's first wife, according to 1 Samuel 18:27, and 1 Chronicles 3:4-9 tells us that David had seven more wives and had children with them as well as with his concubines. We also read about God taking wives from their husbands and giving them to other men (see Jeremiah 8:10, 2 Samuel 12:8, 2 Samuel 12:11-12).

I certainly don't cite these examples as an effort to reinstitute multiple wives or harems of concubines. I do so to show that marriage is a legal matter, and the laws of the day, culture, and land determine what marriage is and what it is not. Marriage legislation in some cultures gives legal protection to women. In Bible times, legal marriage determined which of a man's children were to receive an inheritance, and it could remove a man from the duty of providing for a woman if she had sexual relations with a man other than her husband.

We learn in Genesis 38 that it was the duty of a brother to impregnate his brother's wife if that man died before they had a child together. This was a protection set up for women who were married so that they would have some family for support in addition to providing an heir to the brother who had died.

So when Jesus said we won't be married in heaven, it's at the very least because of all the complex laws and situations that we have developed after we fell away from God's original intent. Marriage itself has many purposes today that would have been unnecessary in the sinless, perfect world of Eden.

Male and Female Relationships in Heaven

In my opinion, because the Bible tells us God will restore humans rather than diminish them, the male and female relationship of God's original intent will be brought back, redeemed and restored, rather than being removed as some suggest. However, because Jesus states that there will be no marriage as we know it now, I don't know how to explain it past that point. To what extent we could see relationships between men and women restored I'll leave to your own thought and study.

It seems possible, however, that the "new" humans will have a choice on the New Earth whether or not they will be with their spouses from this life. Remember that in Matthew 22:30 the Pharisees tried to trick Jesus by asking him who would be married to a widow of seven husbands at the resurrection. That's when Jesus told them that they didn't know "the Scriptures or the power of God," and told them that people wouldn't marry in heaven.

From what Jesus said, we can know that we won't be held to the laws of this current earth, meaning we won't be bound to our spouse from this life. However, it's a sure bet that many will want to be in a relationship with their spouses from this life. Without the sin and frustrations of this life, a relationship with our spouse from this life could be an incredible bond. Then again, I think it's realistic to say that others might want to go their separate ways on the New Earth. The bottom line is that it was God's idea to create us male and female. Heaven is a *restoration* of God's original intent, as we're told in Acts 3:21 and Romans 8; therefore, I think it's possible and even probable that romantic capacity will be restored and perhaps be even stronger than in this present life.

It's certainly not unreasonable to think that in heaven we would have a special connection with the person we were married to during this life. We'll have so much history with that person that having a strong relationship on the New Earth is not a far-fetched concept. So if you're having difficulty thinking we could have romantic relationships on the New Earth, start by considering what it will be like to see your spouse for the first time in the next life. The two of you will be without physical problems, without the stress that currently weights us down at nearly every turn, and without the misunderstandings and grudges that might have been brought on by circumstances of life on the fallen earth. The potential for a better relationship would be extraordinary in God's restored paradise!

This chapter might raise more questions than it answers, and that's fine. Just know that God is able to work everything out as it should be. We can confidently place it all in his hands and trust him with what will be.

Through my years of working with troubled marriages, I've observed most of the problems caused by the godlessness of this earth; but I've also seen the magnificence of the love that can be shared by a man and woman because God gave us that capability. To whatever extent we'll experience that relationship again, you'll see glimpses of it in those times when you and your spouse love unselfishly, put the needs of each other above one's own, fulfill each other, laugh with each other, and embrace. So make every effort to give your spouse as many tastes of heaven as possible in your life together.

CHAPTER 10
What Will Keep Us From Sinning Again?

In discussing the restoration of all things as foretold in Acts 3:21, we find ourselves asking this question: If God is going to restore humans to the same state Adam and Eve enjoyed before the fall, what's to stop us from falling again? What will keep us from falling for temptation again and losing paradise just like Adam and Eve?

Deception and Doubt

Satan convinced Eve that God was holding out on her and that she would benefit from disobeying God by eating the fruit of the Tree of Knowledge of Good and Evil.

We know how that turned out.

Death came about for all of creation because of humankind's yielding to Satan's deceit. God wasn't keeping something from us that was good or that would bring us more joy. He was protecting us from death and separation from him and the creation he originally gave us.

I was bitten by a snake as a teenager and I can assure you that one result of that experience is that I am not at all tempted to place my hand in front of a snake again. Not in the least! I don't worry that I'm going to be tempted to let a snake bite me again. I don't have to take it one day at a time or join a support group to discourage me from seeking out a snake to bite me. It is, in fact, the opposite of a temptation; it is revolting and unimaginable. In the same way, we will not want to sin in the next life because we have experienced the tragic pain of sin in this life. We've seen what it did to our relationships, our world, and our bodies. We've watched loved ones die and we've hurt those dear to us because of the sinful nature we contracted.

Though I don't worry that I'll be tempted to let a snake bite me, I could, however, worry that I'll be bitten by a snake I didn't know was there. But that's another great thing about the New Earth: Satan won't be there to tempt us or attempt to harm us in any way.

And the devil, who deceived them, was thrown into the lake of burning sulfur, where the beast and the false prophet had been thrown. They will be tormented day and night forever and ever. (Revelation 20:10)

He who does what is sinful is of the devil, because the devil has been sinning from the beginning. The reason the Son of God appeared was to destroy the devil's work. (1 John 3:8)

Since the children have flesh and blood, he too shared in their humanity so that by his death he might destroy him who holds the power of death—that is, the devil—and free those who all their lives were held in slavery by their fear of death. (Hebrews 2:14-15)

And then the lawless one will be revealed, whom the Lord Jesus will overthrow with the breath of his mouth and destroy by the splendor of his coming. (2 Thessalonians 2:8)

Not only will we have the experience to know that sin brings pain, suffering, and death, but we will also be without the one who deceived us in the first place.

Our True Nature Restored

We have a sinful nature now, but that nature was not within humans at the beginning. The first humans didn't develop a sinful nature until they ate of the fruit of the Tree of Knowledge of Good and Evil. The sinful nature we now have resulted from the severe warping of our original human nature.

The good news is that we'll have a superior nature to that of Adam and Eve because we'll have the righteousness made available to us by the atonement of Jesus Christ.

For just as through the disobedience of the one man the many were made sinners, so also through the obedience of the one man the many will be made righteous. (Romans 5:19)

For Christ did not enter a man-made sanctuary that was only a copy of the true one; he entered heaven itself, now to appear for us in God's presence. Nor did he enter heaven to offer himself again and again, the way the high priest enters the Most Holy Place every year with blood that is not his own. Then Christ would have had to suffer many times since the creation of the world. But now he has appeared once for all at the end of the ages to do away with sin by the sacrifice of himself. (Hebrews 9:24-26)

... by one sacrifice he has made perfect forever those who are being made holy. The Holy Spirit also testifies to us about this. First he says: "This is the covenant I will make with them after that time, says the Lord. I will put my laws in their hearts, and I will write them on their minds." (Hebrews 10:14-15)

Adam and Eve were created innocent and thus holy. Their holiness allowed intimacy with God, but after they sinned that level of intimacy with God was lost.

Whereas the first Adam brought death through what he did, the second Adam, Jesus, brought life through what he did. When Jesus lived on the earth, he did not sin—not even once, though he faced the full force of Satan's temptation. "For we do not have a high priest who is unable to sympathize with our weaknesses, but we have one who has been tempted in every way, just as we are—yet was without sin" (Hebrews 4:15).

He was "without sin" while in his human body because he had something Adam did not have. He had the Holy Spirit dwelling within him.

This was to fulfill what was spoken through the prophet Isaiah: "Here is my servant whom I have chosen, the one I love, in whom I delight; I will put my Spirit on him, and he will proclaim justice to the nations. He will not quarrel or cry out; no one will hear his voice in the streets. A bruised reed he will not break, and a smoldering wick he will not snuff out, till he leads justice to victory. In his name the nations will put their hope." (Matthew 12:17-21)

. . . God anointed Jesus of Nazareth with the Holy Spirit and power . . . . (Acts 10:38)

His nature was pure and undefiled by sin and that allowed him to be the perfect sacrifice to take away our sins. Whereas the Bible tells us that "the wages of sin is death" (Romans 6:23), Jesus experienced death though he had *not* sinned. This conundrum is what allows us to experience eternal life even though we *have* sinned. "God made him who had no sin to be sin for us, so that in him we might become the righteousness of God" (2 Corinthians 5:21).

Because Jesus was able to live in the flesh and not sin or fall for the temptations of Satan, we too will have that ability in our new bodies. The Bible tells us that sin will be put to death (Hebrews 9:26). Therefore, sin will be like a disease that has been completely eradicated from the planet. You won't have to make special efforts to keep from being infected because you can't contract what's not there!

Do We Lose Freedom of Choice if We Can't Sin?

When I speak on this topic, the question is often asked, "If we no longer have sin as an option, do we lose our freedom of choice or free moral agency?" I understand why it's being asked, but I believe the question is incorrect. Being without sin is not the same as being without choice or freedom.

After all, God cannot sin because his nature is to be holy. God also can't learn anything new (he's omniscient), stop existing (he's everlasting), change his nature (Malachi 3:6), or lie (Titus 1:2, Hebrews 6:18), but we wouldn't suggest that he is without free choice.

I can't spin a web like a spider, but does that mean I don't have freedom of choice? No, it's just not natural for me to spin a web like a spider. When we are transformed into who God made us to be through Christ, it won't be natural for us to sin.

The freedom we will have is that we will be freed *from* sin and its consequences. We'll be free of all the terrible things that sin has brought on us.

... through Christ Jesus the law of the Spirit of life set me free from the law of sin and death. (Romans 8:2)

It is for freedom that Christ has set us free. Stand firm, then, and do not let yourselves be burdened again by a yoke of slavery. (Galatians 5:1)

They promise them freedom, while they themselves are slaves of depravity—for a man is a slave to whatever has mastered him. (2 Peter 2:19)

Now the Lord is the Spirit, and where the Spirit of the Lord is, there is freedom. (2 Corinthians 3:17)

. . . the creation itself will be liberated from its bondage to decay and brought into the glorious freedom of the children of God. (Romans 8:21)

Reasons We Will Not Sin Again

The seer of Revelation wrote: "And I heard a loud voice from the throne saying, 'Now the dwelling of God is with men, and he will live with them. They will be his people, and God himself will be with them and be their God'" (Revelation 21:3). As we discussed earlier, God is bringing heaven to the New Earth, whereas in the days of Adam and Eve (and currently) heaven's location was elsewhere in the universe. God's dwelling place will be with our dwelling place and his presence won't allow sin even to be near. We will be able to live as he originally intended—without sin.

But many thoughtful people ask how we can have free will but not be able to sin. If we have free will, what's to stop us from falling into temptation again?

There are at least five reasons why we won't sin on the New Earth.

1. We will have learned that God was not deceiving us by telling us that sin caused death. Satan was the one deceiving us and we'll know better.

2. Satan won't be around. Satan will not be able to tempt us because he'll be locked away in permanent punishment. "And the devil, who deceived them, was thrown into the lake of burning sulfur, where the beast and the false prophet had been thrown. They will be tormented day and night forever and ever" (Revelation 20:10).

3. We will have our true nature protected by the righteousness of Christ, which means we won't sin because it will not be our nature.

4. Sin will not exist because Jesus died to destroy it. We can't contract a nonexistent disease.

5. We will forever be in the presence of God and sin cannot exist in God's holy presence.

We need not be concerned that we could fall again. God will keep us standing and holy on the New Earth. We don't even need all five of the reasons listed above. God destroying sin through Jesus was enough. We will never again have to face life separated from God because of sin!

Our nature and purpose was to have fellowship with God forever. What Satan killed, Jesus resurrected, and his power will sustain us permanently.

CHAPTER 11
Is It Important to Study Heaven?

Though I don't have all the answers, I wanted to share with you the benefits of our studies in this book. I also want to encourage you to study these things for yourself. Study God's Word and reach your own conclusions.

One of the main lessons to take from this book is that Satan does not want us to be reunited with God, each other, and God's creation. From the beginning of human existence, Satan has done everything in his power to convince people to be their own gods and to ignore the true God. Satan is not going to stop until everyone has made his or her decision concerning God and God locks Satan away for eternity.

That is why it is important for us to educate ourselves concerning God's plans for heaven. We are going to have to stand against Satan's lies and misunderstandings caused by his deception. To do that, some of us may have to make some changes.

We Must Change Our Attitudes

"Can you help my marriage?" She asked in a trembling voice.

Before I could answer, she calmly said, "I only have about a year to live. I just want some precious moments with my husband before I die."

She told me of how her husband reacted to the news of her terminal illness with total denial. "He's mean to me and complains when he takes me for my treatments. It seems my illness has become a tremendous burden in his life, and he seems to resent me for it. I guess all I have to look forward to now is heaven."

The way she said it left me at a loss for words. By the tone of her voice, I could tell that she felt the sad part of all this was that she actually *had* to look forward to heaven. All the better options, like living on in this life, had been taken away from her.

I must admit that I've felt that way in the past, and I certainly don't want to be critical of people in such difficult situations; but I think Christians should stop viewing heaven as a consolation prize. As we have seen, this life is important. While we should not seek death or dismiss ourselves from the responsibilities of this life, we must change our attitudes concerning heaven.

I believe that many of our struggles in life are because of Satan's efforts to steal us away from God. He wants us to reject God, not only because Satan hates us, but also because he hates God and wants to take God's children away in order to hurt him. Satan has a massive amount of experience in deceiving humankind that dates back to the very first humans. He studies us and tries to use our weaknesses against us.

A basic tool of Satan is false information and lies. The Bible calls him the "father of lies" in John 8:44. It was Satan who convinced Eve that God was somehow holding out on her.

Revelation 13:6 tells us that Satan "opened his mouth to blaspheme God, and to slander his name and his dwelling place and those who live in heaven." Note that Satan slanders three things: God himself, God's people, and God's "dwelling place," heaven.

If Satan can fool non-Christians into believing that the Bible teaches that heaven consists of ghosts floating around in the clouds in a boring and impersonal abstraction, fewer people will want to consider how they can go there.

Furthermore, if Satan can convince Christians of those same misconceptions concerning heaven, he has a good chance of dampening their passion to lead people to God. We need to help fellow Christians understand the biblical picture of heaven to keep that from happening.

In past conversations with other Christians about the next life, I remember hearing people say the same thing that I was taught as a teenager: "The main thing is that no matter what heaven will be like, it will be better than hell." Sadly, their main reason for accepting Jesus as their savior was *not* that they wanted to be with God forever but that they were terrified of hell.

Please don't misunderstand. I believe that a good, healthy fear of hell is a strong motivator for taking our dedication to God seriously. But I also believe that if we only choose heaven as an alternative to hell, we are selling God short and dooming ourselves to a lackluster faith that won't inspire anyone around us to choose salvation.

After all, I can think of *lots* of things that are better than hell that I wouldn't want to experience for eternity. Examples include root canals, paying taxes, having headaches, packing for moves, facing editors when book manuscripts are overdue, and having car trouble. I'd rather experience any of those things than hell, but I certainly do not look forward to any of those things. I don't get excited about those things.

When Christians begin teaching that God has, through the sacrifice of Jesus, redeemed not only humans, but also the earth and all creation to restore it to perfect form, our fears of the next life will subside and we will be much better witnesses for Christ.

We should start by teaching that heaven is far more than a consolation prize, but rather the true desire of our minds, bodies, and spirits.

Heaven will help us be better friends, sons, and daughters. It will enable us to show and feel love more deeply and intensely. The resurrection of our bodies and the restoration of the earth is what we long for when we see the new wrinkles appearing on our foreheads or when we watch a casket lowered into the ground. It's what we instinctively know we're missing when we have to swallow a pill to keep from hurting. Heaven is the ultimate gift, the ultimate incentive, and the ultimate destination. It's where our dreams can become reality and where we can make up for lost time with those we love. Leaving this out of our message to the lost would be a nonsensical mistake.

I realize this book has likely been a lot to consider and may have been a challenge to what you've been taught all your life about heaven. Some of you might be trying to keep up with all the details discussed in this book and feel unprepared to explain to others what the Bible teaches heaven will be like. The central theme of this book comes from Acts 3:21. We have mentioned it several times in this book so that it will be more likely to lodge in your memory: "He must remain in heaven until the time comes for God to restore everything, as he promised long ago through his holy prophets."

An easy-to-understand explanation can start with that passage. The bottom line is that God is going to restore the earth and humans to his original intent as it was before the fall. We're not going to be placed in some other realm or be another creature altogether. We'll be different and better humans, but humans nonetheless. We'll live the eternal lives that humans were supposed to live—free from sickness, death, and sin and in intimate fellowship with God, each other, and creation.

The other passage that expands on Acts 3:21 and echoes throughout this book is Romans 8:18-23.

I consider that our present sufferings are not worth comparing with the glory that will be revealed in us. The creation waits in eager expectation for the sons of God to be revealed. For the creation was subjected to frustration, not by its own choice, but by the will of the one who subjected it, in hope that the creation itself will be liberated from its bondage to decay and brought into the glorious freedom of the children of God.

We know that the whole creation has been groaning as in the pains of childbirth right up to the present time. Not only so, but we ourselves, who have the firstfruits of the Spirit, groan inwardly as we wait eagerly for our adoption as sons, the redemption of our bodies.

The entire universe was thrown into havoc due to the fall of humankind. But the Bible tells us that God is going to redeem both us and all of creation from that fall. He is going to set things back to how he created them and will remove the deceiver.

If you can explain that much, you'll be on your way to helping others understand the concept of heaven and the New Earth as the Bible truly teaches.

Can We Know That We Are Going to Heaven

I remember having a terrible dream as a teenager. The dream was so bad that I woke screaming and lay awake in bed until daylight. I had dreamed about judgment day, but not the one for which I'd hoped. In the dream, I watched from my window as Jesus took people from their homes to be with him. I waited for Jesus to come for me, but he did not. He eventually disappeared in the distance. The earth became eerily silent and in the distance I could see someone else.

It wasn't Jesus returning for me.

As the monstrously gigantic figure grew closer, I could tell who it was.

Satan.

We made eye contact, and I ran to hide. Somehow I ended up face down on my bed, praying for God to come back and save me, when suddenly the walls of the house rumbled as though in a massive earthquake. I felt the house rising toward the sky and looked out the window to see smoke. I ran to the window and peered outside to see the face of Satan. Fire covered the ground like a river, and the flames wrapped around him. He held my house in the palm of his hand and with his other hand he reached into the window to capture me.

That's when I awoke with a scream.

I've been through tornados, car wrecks, and gun fire, but those experiences cannot compare to the terror that paralyzed my body after that nightmare. The dream revealed my heart at the time. I didn't know what would happen to me if I died because my relationship with God had been suffering.

A few months later, I listened to a sermon on salvation and its words deeply refreshed me. Especially the words of 1 John 5:13: "I write these things to you who believe in the name of the Son of God so that you may know that you have eternal life." The Holy Spirit inspired John to write those words so that we can know we have eternal life. Not so that we'll "have the best shot at it" or so that we'll "feel a little better about it," but so that we can *know* we are going to heaven to be with God.

It's more important for your name to be written in the Book of Life than it is for you to know exactly what heaven will be like. It's also important that you know you are going to be with God so that when you speak to others you will speak with confidence and experience.

Jesus said, "I am the way and the truth and the life. No one comes to the Father except through me" (John 14:6). In this day, it's popular to consider ourselves too enlightened to believe such a narrow claim. We don't want to appear judgmental, and we don't want to be considered bigots.

Nevertheless, it's dangerous for us to base our beliefs on what is politically correct or simply popular at any given time.

If we truly believed there are lost people on the earth, then we would be bolder in approaching them about Jesus. We wouldn't wait around, thinking that they will eventually be won over because we didn't "push our religion" on them. We also wouldn't be so timid that we rationalize our lack of personal evangelism by saying that we would have more influence on people by waiting until they ask us.

Jesus certainly didn't wait to be asked. Many times his comments brought people to ask questions. He volunteered information to those within his influence many times without waiting for questions. His boldness often drew crowds around him.

Likewise, we need to be bold and confident so that we can bring people to heaven with us. I'm certainly not saying we should be rude or annoying, but we undoubtedly need to share the message of salvation by our words and actions as we live on this earth. Our willingness to share (or not) will have eternal significance.

Conclusion

None of our accomplishments on this earth mean much if we are not on God's side when the Day of Judgment comes. Death comes for us all unless Jesus returns during our lifetimes. Though we might try to buy time in a bottle, no amount of vitamins, minerals, medicine, or exercise can prevent it from eventually happening.

God offers to give us our lives back! He is willing to forgive and forget the fall of man and restore things to the way he intended in the beginning when everything was youthful and fresh.

How could we possibly refuse his offer?

Live this life so that you will be with Jesus in heaven. Conduct yourself around your friends and family so that you can have precious moments, long conversations, and great adventures with them in heaven on the New Earth.

I hope to see you there!

The True Heaven Study Guide

Introduction
An Explanation of How Dread Turned to Hope

1. The introduction says, "I was terrified by the entire concept of heaven." Have you ever felt that way? If yes, what about the concept terrified or repelled you?

2. Do you think Christians discuss the topic of heaven enough, too much, or just the right amount? Why do you think that?

3. What times or events in life cause you to look forward to heaven?

Chapter 1:
The Myth of Heaven

1. Have you ever heard some of the myths about heaven discussed in this chapter? If so, which ones and what were your thoughts about them?

2. Do you feel that with the current societal fascination with immortality and spiritual creatures Christians could use the message of heaven to provide the answer to the desires of people's hearts?

3. Do you often think of heaven as the "parting gift" for dying? How has this book helped you see heaven differently?

Chapter 2:
Heaven Is an Actual Place

1. According to John 14:2 Jesus left to prepare a place for us. What does this passage mean to you?

2. I cannot imagine a more appropriate job for the Creator of the earth and stars than carpentry." Do you agree with this statement? Why or why not?

3. Why do you think the Bible provides us with "previews" of heaven rather than keeping it a complete secret?

Chapter 3:
Who Will Be In Heaven?

1. In your own words, explain how someone who was never taught the laws of God could have them in their heart.

2. How do you think the Jewish people in the first century reacted to Paul reminding them that other people kept God's law without being Jewish or even knowing of their existence? Do you think some might react in that same way to some of the words of this chapter?

3. How do you feel about potentially seeing some of your enemies in heaven? Do you think your attitude is in line with God's?

Chapter 4:
What Will We Be in Heaven?

1. What about human beings make us different from angels? From animals? From God?

2. What three parts combine to make a complete human being?

3. Why do you think Jesus wanted the disciples and future readers of the Bible to know that he was not a ghost? (See Luke 24:37-39)

4. What does the Bible mean when it calls Jesus the "first fruits" of the resurrection (1 Corinthians 15:20)?

5. Why do you think Jesus retained the scars on his hands in his resurrection body?

6. Do you feel comfort in the message of this book concerning the recognition of friends and family members in heaven?

7. According to Revelation 21, why will our new bodies not experience old age or deterioration?

8. What is a central belief of Gnosticism as discussed in this chapter? Why do you think so many Christians unknowingly believe Gnostic teachings as some did in Paul's day?

Chapter 5:
What Happens When Humans Die?

1. Do you struggle with the concept of death?

2. Do you pray for God to comfort you about this fear?

3. Have you ever experienced an event like the one that happened to Todd? If not, do you believe such events could occur?

4. Do you feel encouraged to know that "a great cloud of witnesses" watch us run our Christian race? (Hebrews 12)

5. What does the Bible mean when it tells us to "set [our] minds on things above" but then tells us to take this life seriously as well? What are ways we can combine these two concepts?

Chapter 6:
Where Is Heaven?

1. What are the three uses of the word "heaven" in the Bible?

2. Why should we be leery of anyone who claims to know the exact location of heaven?

3. Do you agree with the assumption that heaven is somewhere in the universe because Jesus left for heaven by ascending rather than disappearing. Why or why not?

Chapter 7:
Life on the New Earth

1. This chapter tells a story about a dad teaching his son to drive by first having him drive in an empty parking lot. The message

is that God expects us to give proper focus to the little things in this life so that we can be trusted with larger responsibilities in this life and in heaven. How do you think we can do this? What things in this life might prepare us for heaven?

2. In what ways is life on earth different from God's original intent?

3. In what ways do you struggle with the temptation to be your own god? What are you doing to put your trust in God and not in your own abilities and efforts?

4. This chapter discusses loving "this world" while at the same time understanding that we are to separate ourselves from this world in its present form. How can we do this?

5. Before reading this chapter, did you imagine a heaven with absolutely no work or tasks? If so, why? In what way, if any, has your view changed?

6. What do you think 1 Corinthians 6:2 means? What about 2 Timothy 2:12?

7. Why do you think it is not popular to discuss different rewards and responsibilities in heaven?

Chapter 8:
Will Animals Be in Heaven?

1. After reading this chapter, do you think animals will be in heaven?

2. What do you think Romans 8:19-22 means?

3. In what ways did God establish a covenant with animals?

4. To whom do animals belong?

5. If you've lost a pet to death, how does this chapter make you feel?

Chapter 9:
Will We Be Male and Female in Heaven?

1. If you are married, do you feel you are giving your spouse "heaven on earth" as described in this chapter? If not, will you commit to finding the right tools to enable yourself to do that? (Remember that JoeBeam.com provides resources to strengthen marriage relationships even when they're severely troubled.)

2. What did you think your relationship with your spouse would be like in heaven before you read this chapter? If your view has changed after reading this chapter, how has it changed?

3. Do you agree that a restoration of the original male and female romance makes sense based on Acts 3:21 and other passages that speak of God restoring things to His original intent? Why or why not?

4. Compare your thoughts on this topic prior to reading this chapter. In what ways were they different and in what ways are they the same?

Chapter 10:
What Will Keep Us From Sinning Again?

1.   What are five reasons that we won't sin again on the New Earth.

2.   Explain how we can be free but not have the ability to sin.

3.   Explain how we will be in an even better situation than Adam and Eve in regard to protecting our sinless human nature.

Chapter 11:
Is It Important to Study Heaven?

1.   Do you think it is important to study heaven?

2.   What three things does Revelation 13:6 tell us Satan blasphemes/slanders? Why do you think he does this?

3.   Have you ever had a nightmare like the one described in this chapter? What happened in your nightmare?

4. According to 1 John 5:13, why did John write the things he mentioned in the book of 1 John?

5. In what ways can we teach our friends about God's offer of eternal life?

Internet Resources

By Joe and Lee

For Marriage Relationships:

www.JoeBeam.com

www.MarriageHelper.com

For Discussion and Bible Study Tools:

www.GraceCentered.com/forums

For Christian Singles:

www.RealChristianSingles.com